Hannibal
The Greatest General

The Meteoric Rise, Defeat, and Destruction of Rome's Fiercest Rival

By Barry Linton

Copyright 2015 by Barry Linton.

Published by Make Profits Easy LLC

Profitsdaily123@aol.com

facebook.com/MakeProfitsEasy

Table of Contents

Foreword 4

Chapter 1: Origins of a Great Leader 8

Chapter 2: Battle of Saguntum 14

Chapter 3: A Nation at War 19

Chapter 4: Leading the Armies of Carthage 31

Chapter 5: A Man Set Apart 45

Chapter 6: Man Becomes Myth 54

Chapter 7: Crossing the Alps............................. 67

Chapter 8: The Die is Cast 86

Chapter 9: The Retreat of Rome 102

Chapter 10: The Battle of Cannae 114

Chapter 11: Pyrrhus of Epirus 128

Chapter 12: To the Gates of Rome 146

Chapter 13: The Legacy of Scipio 166

Chapter 14: One Must Fall 177

Chapter 15: Nothing Lasts Forever 209

Conclusion..218

Foreword

Hannibal Barca of Carthage had been a military leader, statesman, and staunch defender of his people. When he was young, he learned the importance of accountability. He grew to appreciate his people, and under the tutelage of his father became a mighty warrior and great commander of men. He accomplished outstanding triumphs in opposition to the Romans, frequently fighting at a significant disadvantage. He led his people through the Second Punic War and beyond, until their final devastation at the hands of the Romans.

This book chronicles his adventures. He accomplished many great successes, experienced personal tragedies, and yet persevered through it all. He's a polarizing character in history, and continues to be mysterious. Many documents of his exploits were most likely destroyed or altered by the conquering Romans, but what remains of his story has been studied by historians for a very long time. His great strategic victories and stunning crossing of the Alps have been esteemed by modern-day military leaders. Hannibal is considered to be one of the most brilliant generals in history, fathering many strategies that would later be applied by leaders such as Napoleon.

While the Roman historians would understandably be biased toward the Carthaginian general, there remain some clues about his personality and character. Roman historians generally portray him as being cruel and filled with blood lust but under further examination this can be contested. On one particular occasion he entered into an agreement with Fabius Cunctator for the release and return of prisoners of war. He also treated the bodies of the fallen Consuls Gracchus and Paulus with dignity and respect before returning them to the Romans. He has also been accused of avarice, but his frequent attempts to make money and increase his fortunes are understandable when the costs of financing a mercenary army are considered. This can also be attributed to the generally poor financial conditions that his father commanded through. Many accounts required him to be brave and unafraid of placing himself in danger when necessary. He was willing to fight alongside his men and on more than one occasion used himself as bait, to great success. The fact that he led a mercenary army comprised of such a wide variety of nationalities and backgrounds for so long is a tribute to his powers of leadership and charisma. His strategies show wit and subtlety. While most personal information about him was likely destroyed along with Carthage, we do know that he spoke Greek and Latin fluently. Considering the broad background of his soldiers and his penchant for treating his soldiers humanely, he may have learned even more languages.

His multitude of victories over the Romans while in hostile territory over a span of 15 years cemented his position in history. At the same time this sealed the relentless efforts of the Romans to eradicate the Carthaginian people. Hannibal ultimately played the role of both protector and harbinger for the Carthaginian people.

Chapter 1: Origins of a Great Leader

Hannibal's father proved to be the greatest teacher he could have had, other than personal experience. He learned many tactics firsthand, as he accompanied his father on campaign during the First Punic War. Hannibal was only nine at the time. It is a testament to his own personal qualities as well as the abilities cultivated in him by his father, that he was unanimously chosen to be the Carthaginian general at the age of 26. Hannibal is widely respected and studied because the qualities of his leadership and the cornerstones of his tactics are still applicable today. His early success in the Second Punic War was made possible by two important principles that remain vital in any age of war. These principles are maintaining the element of surprise, and always seizing the initiative.

After the First Punic War, Rome felt safe from any incursions by the Carthaginians. They pressured the Carthaginians and at times tried to goad them into war, and this they did not only because of their hatred toward the Carthaginians, because they believed they were safe from effective counterattack. Hannibal was shrewd and courageous. His initial steps in the second Punic war are akin with what would be expected from modern-day commanders. He secured and fortified his existing bases at Carthage and Carthagena. He then set to collecting detailed information about all lands through which he would need to pass. He sent hand-picked officers to each of these different lands to gather information about the people and customs and terrain and fertility of their country. He also had them gather information about the Alps and about the seasons and when the weather was most favorable. He knew where he could resupply, where he could rest, and for how long. Hannibal is an ancient example of a general who understood the vital importance of logistics and preparedness.

Hannibal Barca was very much his father's son. Raised in the art of war since his early childhood, he was a natural successor to the Barca family. Despite his aptitude, a rift was growing between Carthage and the Barcas in Spain. He was a product of the teachings of his father, Hamilcar. He left North Africa at the young age of 9, and his formative years had been spent primarily among the soldiers waging war in Spain.

With the appointment of Hannibal, the perception that the Spanish command was a Barcid family legacy was confirmed. In his account Livy emphasized the sense of resentment towards the Barcids that had built up among some of the Carthaginian political elite, in a diatribe supposedly delivered by Hamilcar's old enemy Hanno in the Carthaginian Council of Elders.

It is clear from the Barcid coinage of this period that Hannibal was keen to promote his familial links with Hamilcar. A series of silver coinage issues appeared showing a portrait of Hercules–Melqart depicted with a number of elements associated with the Greek Hercules, including a club resting on his shoulder and a laurel wreath. The figure is a clean-shaven young man, and on the reverse is an African elephant. At roughly the same time a double-shekel silver coin was released which showed a similar figure with laurel wreath and club. Although this Melqart displays very similar characteristics, he sports a beard and is clearly older. On the reverse there is again an African elephant, but here with a driver on its back. These coins are a progression from earlier coins depicting Melqart, in that they attempt to associate the Barcids and the god. The war elephant was a symbol that came to be increasingly linked with the Barcids during this period. Hellenistic kings and leaders had long blurred the division between personal and divine portraiture. There often appears to be an almost deliberate ambiguity between the human and the divine in the portraits on the coins of Alexander and his successors, which bolstered the issuers' claims to divine protection and favor.

In the Barcid context there also appears to be the added focus on articulating the legitimacy of Hannibal taking command as Hamilcar Barca's son. That legitimacy over the Spanish realm was further bolstered when, as his predecessor Hasdrubal had done, Hannibal married an Iberian woman, from Castulo, 'a powerful and famous city', which was in close alliance with the Barcids. Hannibal spent the first two years of his generalship mopping up opposition and expanding Barcid territory towards the north-west of Spain. He would soon prove his genius as a military commander. Not only did he storm a number of important Celtiberian strongholds, but he also showed great cunning in his destruction of a dangerous enemy force.

In the spring of 220 BC, finding themselves threatened by a formidable foe, Hannibal and his army feigned retreat by crossing the river Tagus and set up camp on its left bank. The trap was now baited by leaving enough space between his trenches and the banks of the river to encourage the enemy to attack. When the enemy started to cross the river, they found themselves under attack from the Barcid cavalry. Those who managed to struggle across found forty of Hannibal's war elephants waiting to trample them underfoot. Hannibal then crossed the river with the rest of his army to deliver the coup de grâce. This victory was so emphatic that others now knew not to test the military worth of the young general.

Chapter 2: Battle of Saguntum

Another important step that Hannibal took was to gather information about the indigenous populations capacities for war. He wanted to know how they felt about the Romans and whether there was any hatred or common ground he could exploit and use to his advantage. He sought an alliance with the Gauls because he knew they would be important to his surprise attack on the Romans over the Alps. He was politically intelligent and adept at securing aid. Using his superior tactical talent, he planned the campaign in which he would gather his supporters and fellow enemies of Rome under one banner and launch a surprise attack against the Romans in the place the least expected.

Hannibal now held much of the territory north of the river Hiberus, with the important exception of the city of Saguntum, which a few years previously had reacted to the creeping northward advance of the Barcids by entering into an alliance with Rome. The Saguntines proved a useful source of information about Barcid activity in Spain, and the relationship was evidently close enough for Roman envoys to be invited to adjudicate when pro-Roman and pro-Barcid factions clashed within the city. Unsurprisingly, the Romans found in favor of the pro-Roman party, and a number of Barcid supporters were executed. The message was clear—any attack on Saguntum would be viewed in Rome as a serious provocation. Undeterred, over the next few months in 220 Hannibal slowly tightened his control over the territory around the city. Alarmed, the Saguntines sent increasingly persistent requests for assistance from their ally Rome. Eventually, after much prevarication, the Roman Senate dispatched envoys to parley with the Barcid general. Once again the Carthaginian Council of Elders was sidelined as the Roman embassy made its way directly to Spain. The meeting that was held in the great palace at New Carthage was very different from the one six years previously, when the hard-pressed Romans had played for time. The young general was solemnly warned not to attempt anything that would harm Rome's ally Saguntum, as its citizens lay within Roman trust.

It was perhaps the hypocrisy of the ambassador's pious reference to Roman fides which riled Hannibal into retaliation. The young general retorted that Rome itself had not delayed in interfering in the affairs of Saguntum, including the driving out and execution of pro-Carthaginian members of its elite. He then bitterly turned the whole question of faithfulness back on to the Romans: 'The Carthaginians, he said, would not overlook this violation of good faith, for it was from old the principle of Carthage never to neglect the cause of the victims of injustice.' Hannibal did not even deign to mention the second Roman demand, that he respect Hasdrubal's agreement not to cross the Hiberus, and he dismissed the envoys–who then sailed to Carthage to make their protests there.

Hannibal's rather high-handed treatment of the Roman ambassadors surely gives an indication of his growing confidence in the Barcid position in Spain. After all, the resources at his disposal were greater than any Carthaginian general had previously enjoyed. Hannibal now controlled almost half of the Iberian Peninsula, an area of roughly 230,000 square kilometers. He had inherited an excellent fighting force of 60,000 infantry, 8,000 cavalry and 200 elephants, honed by over sixteen years of campaigning against a determined and ferocious enemy. A series of alliances had been signed with the leaders of powerful Celtiberian tribes that added to his military strength.

Huge mining production meant that there was enough money to meet war costs. A later Roman writer estimated that one mine at Baebelo, whose shafts ran for more than a Roman mile and half into the mountain, produced an enormous 135 kg of silver a day for Hannibal. Indeed the weight and purity of the silver coinage that was being produced for the troops was a reflection of robust economic health. It was perhaps with these great resources in mind that Hannibal now decided to defy Rome and attack Saguntum. The Saguntines resisted doggedly, and progress was very slow. They made particularly good use of the falarica, a type of oversized javelin, whose meter-long iron spike was bound with material covered in flammable pitch and sulfur and then set ablaze and hurled down on to the Punic attackers. Hannibal himself was wounded in the thigh by a javelin when he strayed too close to the city walls. Not long after, a new Roman embassy landed a short distance away from the Carthaginian camp, but Hannibal refused even to grant them an audience, explaining that he could not guarantee their safety and that he was in any case too busy commanding the siege.

Chapter 3: A Nation at War

The Romans resorted to defensive tactics, and this allowed Hannibal to easily seize the initiative. They avoided a direct confrontation but over time succeeded and gradually reduced Hannibal's ability to wage war. The Romans ultimately launched a campaign in Spain in an attempt to take Hannibal's lands and drive out their Spanish support. Hannibal's brother successfully escaped from Spain and into Italy but was defeated and killed. The Romans slowly took back all of the land that they lost in Italy and this caused Hannibal support to dwindle. When the Romans finally invaded North Africa, Hannibal was recalled to defend. This left him at a disadvantage and he battled and was defeated by Scipio Africanus. Carthage surrendered and this marked the end of the Second Punic War.

After the first Punic war, Carthage main goal was to rebuild economically. Hannibal's father focused on controlling Spain and exploiting the vast mineral resources it contained. He used the money from his ventures to build an Army. Hannibal took over the reins from his father and continued his work. This is where Hannibal began to show his true skill in keening allies and support. He wreaked havoc all across Italy under extremely harsh conditions. He was unmatched and undefeated until Scipio. Even though the Romans often had numerically superior forces that were greatly experienced, to that point Hannibal managed to defeat them all. The Romans however eventually wore him down. Conducting war on enemy soil put Hannibal's Army to their limits. Hannibal could not receive the necessary reinforcements and supplies from Carthage that he needed, so he was forced to subsist off of the lands.

Knowing that the Roman embassy would now again journey on to Carthage, Hannibal sent messengers with a letter addressed to the heads of the Barcid party there, warning them and requesting that they prevent his opponents in the Council of Elders from making any concessions to Rome. Hannibal's action here suggests that, despite the strength of the pro-Barcid faction in Carthage, he feared that some members of the Council of Elders might have been swayed by what the Roman envoys had to say. When one looks at the debased coinage still being minted in the North African metropolis in this period (against the magnificent silver issues being produced in Spain), it could be argued that the beneficial effects of the Barcid economic miracle had not yet reached Carthage.

There were also signs that the alternative policy of developing Carthage's African territory—the strategy that had been pushed by Hanno and his supporters—was beginning to pay dividends. Indeed, archaeological survey of Carthage's African hinterland has revealed an increase in its occupation and agricultural production levels, with considerable amounts of produce being exported from the city to western

Sicily. Tyrrhenian trade was also booming, with large quantities of Campanian black-glaze pottery, which was mostly used as common tableware, being found in Carthage during this period. Certainly some of the more perceptive members of the Roman Senate appear to have been aware of the tensions between the Barcids and some in the Carthaginian Council of Elders, and to have actively sought to exploit those differences. Hannibal was thus perhaps mindful of the importance of bringing Barcid Spain completely back into the Carthaginian fold, to remove any danger of being disowned as a renegade. Most importantly of all, however, he would have wished for the diplomatic agreements that his father and brother-in-law had entered into to be accepted and given the official authority of the Carthaginian state.

In Carthage, the Roman ambassadors at last found somebody who took their complaints and threats seriously. The great Barcid opponent Hanno stood up in front of the Council of Elders and launched a blistering attack on Hannibal. Hanno finished with an exhortation that the siege of Saguntum should be lifted immediately, and Hannibal be handed over to the Romans. But on this occasion his words had little impact, and even his own supporters sat in silence. However, we should be wary of taking this as a ringing endorsement of Barcid unilateralism. Even those councilors who were no friends of the Barcids were still political realists, and if the Carthaginian Council of Elders attempted to relieve Hannibal of his command, that decision would have to be ratified by the Popular Assembly, still very much a Barcid political stronghold.

It also remained to be seen how a man who commanded such a huge standing army and controlled the resources of an area greater than Carthage's African territories could be dismissed and detained. Such a move might momentarily appease Rome, but the Spanish territories in which so much of Carthage's hopes were invested would surely be lost forever. The native tribes swore their allegiance to the Barcids, not to Carthage. They would certainly not meekly accept a replacement overlord from the ranks of the Carthaginian Council. Confronted by their own impotence, the anti-Barcid faction pragmatically elected to keep their counsel. Hannibal's relationship with some members of the Carthaginian elite clearly remained a marriage of convenience. As the Roman historian Cassius Dio would so astutely point out, 'He was not sent forth in the beginning by the magistrates at home, nor later did he obtain any great assistance from them. Although they were to enjoy no slight glory and benefit from his efforts, they wished rather not to appear to be leaving him in the lurch than to cooperate effectively in any enterprise.'

In regards to Saguntum, however, it appeared that Hannibal's calculation had paid off. Despite the later efforts of Rome's historians to conceal the procrastination, the Roman

Senate debated what should be done about Saguntum until it was too late. As the siege entered its eighth month, there was still no sign of a Roman relief force. The starving people of Saguntum eventually gave up hope and committed mass suicide by incinerating their town. Hannibal split the spoils of war three ways. The captives were handed over to the soldiers to be sold as slaves or ransomed, and the proceeds from the sale of all the looted property were sent back to Carthage. As for the gold and silver, Hannibal set that aside for what lay ahead. In Rome, the Senate was split between those who wanted to declare immediate war on Carthage and those who wished to send another embassy. Although Rome would be able to muster a formidable army –and, more importantly, control the seas– the senators knew that by taking on Hannibal they were now subjecting the city to considerable risk against a large and well-trained force led by an energetic and talented leader. After a debate, it was decided to send a mixed delegation of hawkish and dovish senators to Carthage. Their mission was simple: the Carthaginian councilors were to be asked whether Hannibal had acted on his own initiative or whether the attack on Saguntum had been officially sanctioned. If their answer was the former, then a request would be made that Hannibal be handed over for retribution.

The latter would be treated as a declaration of war. When the Roman ambassadors were led into the Carthaginian Council, they met a united body. The Carthaginian councilors had nominated their most talented orator (whose name is not recorded) to act as their spokesman. He contrived to give a subtle answer to the rather blunt question posed by the Roman delegation. Livy presents the speaker cleverly turning the Council's powerlessness into a virtue. He argued that the treaty that Rome had struck with Hasdrubal, in which the Carthaginian general had agreed not to cross the Hiberus, was invalid, because the Council had not been consulted. On the question of Carthaginian perfidy, the tables were then neatly turned on the Romans, who had of course broken the terms of the treaty that had ended the First Punic War by annexing Sardinia. The Carthaginian spokesman followed this up with the argument that Hannibal had not broken the terms of this treaty, because Saguntum had not been a Roman ally when the treaty had been signed. To prove the point, the relevant sections of the treaty were read out aloud. This rhetorical tour de force was finished off with a searching question for the Roman envoys when he demanded that they tell the assembled Carthaginian councilors what Rome's intentions were.

But the Roman envoys were not interested in entering into dialogue. Fabius, their chief negotiator, stood up and pinched the cloth of his toga between two fingers so that he created a fold as a symbol of the stark choice that the Carthaginians faced, saying, 'We offer you here war or peace: choose which you please.' The

Carthaginians would not be drawn, and they replied that it was for Rome to choose the course. Fabius then smoothed out the fold of his toga, and retorted that it would be war, thereby beginning perhaps the most famous conflict of the ancient world. Few scholars now accept the Polybian line that Hannibal's combative stance was the realization of his father Hamilcar's plan to marshal the resources of Spain and then renew the war with Rome. It is nevertheless true that the Barcids were the main driving force in the growing tensions between Rome and Carthage. It is doubtful whether the Carthaginian Council had the political authority or military capability to force Hannibal from his confrontation with Rome, and in any case the Barcid intervention in Spain had been an economic necessity driven by the need to pay off Carthage's war indemnities and to compensate in the long term for the loss of Sicily and Sardinia.

Economic stability was nevertheless as much about security as prosperity, and opposition to Rome must have been a further motivation for resistance. At the same time, the Spanish command presented an opportunity to the Barcids not only for defense against Rome but also to attack it, and thus to restore Carthaginian military prestige, with which the Barcid self-image had been so intertwined since Hamilcar and the First Punic War. That a potential confrontation with Rome was central to Barcid thinking may be gleaned from the actual organization of the Spanish command, which revolved around little more than war and conquest, and thus military training and the acquisition of booty.

Indeed, the restoration of Carthage's old central-Mediterranean empire appears to have been an important strategic aim once war was declared. The Romans, for their part, had shattered any hope of a sustained status quo with the annexation of Sardinia, and their aggressive, expansionist policy must have been well recognized in Carthage. Whether the Romans actually cared about Saguntum is debatable, judging from the protracted period that it took them to come to its defense. Renewed Roman interest in southern Spain in 220 BC probably had less to do with the protection of small allies than with concern at the growing Barcid influence in the region. The capture of Saguntum gave the hawks within the Roman Senate the opportunity to press for a war which they were highly confident of winning. Even those senators who opposed the move appear to have been less concerned with the prevention of war than with Rome's potential image as an unprovoked aggressor. Indeed, the last Roman embassy sent to Carthage had so presented its terms that the Carthaginian Council could not possibly have complied with them. War between the two powers was now unavoidable.

Chapter 4: Leading the Armies of Carthage

The aftermath of the dramatic declaration of hostilities between Carthage and Rome ended up being anticlimactic. Rome could not launch an assault, because its armies were not yet mobilized, but Hannibal had been already making plans. The military approach that was taking shape in his mind was so bold that the Romans never before once considered it as a feasible plan of action. Mindful of the prolonged ordeal that lay in front, Hannibal wintered his army at New Carthage, and dispatched his Iberian contingents on leave.

He also deployed a significant contingent of his Spanish troops—13,850 infantry, 1,200 cavalry and 870 Balearic slingers—to northern Africa, to 'protect' Carthage and other urban centers in Punic Africa, and perhaps to ensure the continued friendliness of the Carthaginian

Council. In return, a similar quantity of African soldiers were sent to replenish Hannibal's army in Spain. The security of Spain was delegated to his brother Hasdrubal, who was put in command of a force of foot soldiers, slingers as well as twenty-one war elephants. This was an instance not just of protecting the peninsula from Roman attack, but also of encouraging the fickle loyalties of the Spanish native tribes, who could very well take advantage of Hannibal's absence. The overland course to Italy provided Hannibal the element of surprise. It was not that the Roman commanders were not expecting an attack, but alternatively that they in no way imagined that he would attempt to take his army to Italy by way of the Alps.

The consuls for 218 BC were Publius Cornelius Scipio along with the equally blue-blooded Tiberius Sempronius Longus. The Roman plan was simple: Scipio, with 22,000 infantry as well as 2,200 cavalry, was to continue to Spain to deliver the conflict to Hannibal.

Longus, with a combined force of over 27,000 men and a fleet of 160 quinqueremes and 20 lighter boats, was to set in motion an intrusion of Africa. There may be little doubt that the Roman Senate reckoned on their Carthaginian counterparts, true to prior form, speeding to negotiate at the first indication of real trouble.

However, on this occasion, Carthaginian nerve held, and Hannibal himself had no intention of meeting the Roman challenge in Spain. Historians have long pondered over Hannibal's motivations in deciding on the arduous land route to Italy. Potential disaster lurked at almost every step. It meant crossing the two highest mountain chains in Western Europe—the Pyrenees and the Alps—and passing, often uninvited, through the territory of hostile tribes who did not welcome such intrusions. This might have seemed daunting enough, even for an army of highly trained professional soldiers, but once 12,000 extremely reluctant Spanish levies and a troop of African elephants were factored into the equation this mission stretched the realms of possibility. Even though taking the overland route gave Hannibal the invaluable advantage of surprise, it was nevertheless an incredibly risky enterprise, born as much from a lack of viable alternatives as from buccaneering endeavor Carthage may have ruled the waves for over 300 years, but since the disastrous defeat in the First Punic War the western Mediterranean had become a Roman sea. Hannibal himself was a living embodiment of just how much the situation had changed, for it was solely as a land general that he had earned his reputation. Indeed, the Punic fleet in Spain at the start of the Second Punic War consisted of only thirty-seven seaworthy quinqueremes and triremes.

Between them Scipio and Longus had over three times that number of ships. Moreover, the Romans controlled many of the bases and much of the coastline by which any fleet would have had to pass in making its way from Spain to Italy. The brutal truth was that for Hannibal to transport his army to Italy by sea would have been even more hazardous than the land route. There was no other option than to take his army overland through Spain and Gaul, over the Pyrenees and the Alps and into Italy.

Despite his fame as a military leader, one of the keys to the future military success that Hannibal would enjoy was the excellence of his lieutenants, themselves excellent generals. In its diverse make-up of levies and mercenaries, Hannibal's army bore a strong resemblance to the armies of the Hellenistic world. The core of his expeditionary force consisted of experienced troops who had fought under him in Spain for a considerable amount of time. Of these, the majority of the heavily armed line infantry which Hannibal brought to Italy were Libyans from areas of North Africa which were subject to Carthage. Famous for their endurance and agility, they were equipped similarly to Roman legionaries, with large oval or oblong shields, short cutting and stabbing swords, and throwing spears. A large number of infantry also came from Spain. The Iberian Peninsula supplied at least 8,000 infantry and 2,000 cavalry for Hannibal's war effort. Iberian levies from areas of southern Spain which had been pacified by the Barcids over the previous twenty years made up a large part of this contingent. Although many of the Iberian tribes had sworn an oath of allegiance to Hannibal and his predecessor Hasdrubal, their loyalty was not a given.

In 218 BC Hannibal's recruiting sergeants, who had been sent to raise troops for the war against Rome, were roughed up by Oretani and Carpetani tribesmen angered at what they perceived as the Barcid general's excessive demands. The Iberian infantry wore no body armor over their national dress of a white linen tunic with purple borders, although the leather caps that they wore may have afforded some protection. They were armed with a large oval shield, throwing javelins, and swords of which the most common was the dreaded falcata, curved and sharpened on both sides near the point, so that its handler could inflict maximum damage by cutting and thrusting at the same time. The Iberians were joined in Hannibal's army by a small number of their wilder cousins, the black-cloaked Celtiberians and sure-footed Lusitanians, who, as they had not been conquered by the Barcids, had to be paid for their services. Hannibal's force also contained over 1,000 highly specialized mercenaries from the Balearics, who fought as slingers. These troops carried a range of different size slings and shot, depending on the range which was required. The majority of Hannibal's cavalry came from Numidia, whose two main kingdoms were Carthage's neighbors, and bound to it by alliance. The Numidians were renowned as superb horsemen, who controlled their pint-sized ponies without saddle, bit or bridle.

As Hannibal's best cavalry, they would prove to be crucial on a number of occasions. These Spaniards and Africans, who had often fought for years under the Barcid standard and were tied to Hannibal by a personal bond of loyalty, provided the core of his expeditionary force. They were his most effective and exceptional troops, and Hannibal used them sparingly—only when their discipline and experience were needed. All ancient armies required a large number of troops who were dispensable. For the Carthaginians it was the Celts, through whose lands Hannibal would have to pass on the way to Italy, who provided the necessary cannon fodder.

The Celts who fought with Hannibal came mainly from the two largest tribal confederations from the Po valley in Cisalpine Gaul (now northern Italy), and they fought in large numbers at a number of key battles. At Cannae, for example, there were 16,000 Celts in the Carthaginian ranks, with a further 8,000 in reserve. Most appear to have been mercenaries recruited through diplomatic treaties agreed with their chiefs, who along with their noblemen fought as cavalrymen. The majority of the Celts of more humble status fought in the massed infantry ranks, often in the front line and armed with long swords sharpened on both sides and designed for slashing. Rather than fighting in formal regiments, war bands of retainers gathered around charismatic leaders selected for both their courage and their fighting prowess. When one looks at the equipment carried by Celtic fighters, it immediately becomes clear why they suffered such high casualties in battle. In the infantry line they appear to have worn trousers, but generally fought bare-chested. They received some protection from their long oak shields, although some sources suggest that these were very narrow and so left the warriors terribly exposed to the spears, javelins and swords of their opponents.

Although Hannibal would become famous for his use of elephants in battle, it was Alexander the Great who had first introduced them into Mediterranean warfare, having encountered them while campaigning in India. His successors seem to have been equally impressed by the intimidating presence of these giant beasts, to the extent that elephants were used in ever-increasing numbers in set-piece battles. Seleucus I of Syria mobilized 480 elephants—a gift from his new ally the Indian king Chandragupta—at the Battle of Ipsus in 301 BC. It was the 'shock and awe' factor of 3 tons of trumpeting elephant flesh, its huge ears spread out like dark canopies, that made them such a 'must have' for most Hellenistic armies. One terracotta statuette from Asia Minor, which was perhaps a commemoration of the Seleucid king Antiochus' famous victory over the Galatian Celts in 275 BC, shows a war elephant complete with driver and howdah on its back throttling an unfortunate barbarian warrior with its trunk and impaling him with its giant tusks while trampling him underfoot. Yet other evidence throws doubt on their effectiveness as killing machines, and the Romans, for example, never considered it worthwhile to use them on the battlefield. African elephants were considered to be particularly unreliable in battle, often turning on their own side with devastating results when panicked or wounded. In an attempt to prevent this, their drivers carried a metal spike which they were expected to plunge into the soft nape of the elephant's neck with a mallet at the point when they lost control of their charges.

The Carthaginians had first come across battle elephants when fighting against Pyrrhus in Sicily. They had then added elephant troops to their own military arsenal, and used them with some success both in the First Punic War and in subsequent campaigns in North Africa and Spain. For the Barcids the elephant seems to have become an emblem of their power on the Iberian Peninsula: its image appears on many high-value coins minted under the authority of Hasdrubal and Hannibal. The choice of the war elephant for battle was a fitting bridge between the martial aspirations of the Barcid clan and the great Hellenistic tradition of which these great beasts had long been a symbol. But the Barcid use of elephants differed from that of the Hellenistic kings in one important respect, for the former's elephants were not of the larger Asian or bush African variety, but the smaller, now-extinct, forest species which dwelt in the foothills of the Moroccan Atlas mountains and the Rif valley. There has been much academic debate over quite how Hannibal used his elephants on military campaign, other than as a way of intimidating the enemy. Recent research has suggested that, contrary to the previously held orthodoxy, Hannibal's smaller African forest elephants may have been able to carry a howdah with archers, as their larger Indian cousins did. Hannibal's greatest strength as a military commander was his ability to transform what initially appeared to be his major weakness, the lack of homogeneity in his army, to his advantage.

He did not attempt to standardize how his troops fought, but used their variety as a way of offering up a diverse range of military options. Indeed, flexibility was the byword of Hannibal's armies. Tactical orthodoxies were thrown to the wayside as the Carthaginian general frequently bewildered his opponents with new and often rapidly changing formations. Although since the First Punic War the Carthaginian army appears to have adopted the phalanx–the rectangular massed infantry formation that had long been a favorite in the Hellenistic world–Hannibal introduced some important modifications. The long spears and pikes, which could be used effectively only after many years of specialized training, were discarded in favor of heavy-bladed thrusting swords which could be quickly mastered by his assorted body of troops. Moreover, the heavy-infantry phalanx, though undoubtedly an effective bludgeon on the battlefield, could also be unwieldy and slow, and so was customized into a number of different tactical models, including the introduction of a hollow core with the strongest troops deployed on the wings–excellent for effecting an encirclement of the enemy. Conscious of his army's shortcomings, Hannibal managed to transform them into strengths through intelligent generalship. In essence, the Second Punic War was one of the first in which the tactical awareness and abilities of its generals would override other, more conventional, military strengths such as numbers and weapons.

Chapter 5: A Man Set Apart

In his contrast of the Carthaginian and Roman forces at this particular time period, Polybius had been enthusiastic to indicate precisely what he saw as the key distinctions between the armies: 'Carthaginians entirely disregard their infantry, despite the fact that do pay some slight attention to their cavalry. The reason for this is that the troops they pay are foreign and mercenary, whereas that from the Romans happen to be native belonging to the soil and citizens.' Now we have already seen how Polybius differentiated the Roman and Carthaginian forces—the former as comprised mainly of reliable citizen soldiers, the latter of ultimately weaker mercenaries—and exactly how incorrect his depiction was in regards of the Carthaginian army. For the Roman forces too his straight assessment does not stand up to scrutiny. Even though Polybius' examination of the composition of Roman forces may well have been appropriate for his own period, it could not reliably represent the situation in 218. The central foundation of the military without a doubt consisted of Roman citizens, but around fifty percent of the strength of each legion had been supplied by various allied troops, and in quite a few military engagements allied troops outnumbered their citizen counterparts. These types of allies were divided into two broad groups: the Latins and the Italians. The former had long-standing and close associations with Rome, for quite a few of them happened to be descendants of Roman settlers who had forsaken their citizenship for the chance of a more prosperous future. Indeed, the Latin states shared a great deal with Rome, including language, religion and governmental institutions, and their people experienced certain rights under Roman law.

The Italians, however, were a different matter. Many had relatively recently been compelled into becoming 'allies' of Rome, and their loyalty could not be guaranteed. The support of the Celtic tribes in Cisalpine Gaul was therefore extremely important, particularly as the Carthaginian army would be passing through their territory. These peoples were not directly ruled by Rome, and Polybius reports that, when Roman envoys attempted to gain their support after war had been declared against Carthage, the response was hardly favorable, with frequent interruptions and derisive laughter. One of the reasons that the Gauls gave for their unwillingness to come to Rome's aid was that 'they heard that men of their race were being expelled from Italy, and made to pay tribute to Rome, and subjected to every other indignity.' Another potential ally was Rome's eastern neighbor, Macedon. The king, Philip V, was a young man who had ascended to the throne in 221 BC. He had quickly proved that he possessed all the qualities required of anyone who was to make a success of ruling that restless and violent land. A ruthless political operator and shrewd military tactician, Philip had quickly become embroiled in a vicious war against the Aetolians, a powerful political confederation in central Greece. A succession of military victories soon followed, which brought him great plaudits within Greece, including the flattering title of 'darling of Hellas'. However, Philip's plans also involved securing a permanent outlet on to the Adriatic Sea. It was this particular ambition that brought him into direct contact with Rome, and to the attention of Hannibal. At the same time that Hannibal was besieging Saguntum, Rome had made its first intervention into territory which traditionally fell within the Macedonian sphere of influence.

The Romans had previously attempted to maintain influence in the key area of Illyria by supporting a local warlord, Demetrius of Phalerum. By 219, however, the Romans had terminally fallen out with their erstwhile ally, who had set himself up as the pirate prince of the Dalmatian coast and begun to menace Italian shipping. Rome sent a fleet to Illyria and

Demetrius fled, seeking refuge with his other protector, Philip of Macedon.

At the point when Hannibal was starting out upon his great expedition, therefore, several of Rome's key strategic alliances appeared insecure. Hannibal, however, needed equally to guarantee the support of the Punic world, whose enthusiasm for his venture was far from assured. Punic communities in Sicily and Sardinia would need the confidence to rebel against their new Roman masters, especially considering the inevitable high price of defeat. In Carthage, too, the continued support of the Council of Elders was a vital precondition of military success, for Hannibal required not only troops and money from North Africa, but also authority. His ability to attract the support of others required that he be seen as the representative of the Carthaginian state, not just another rootless military adventurer. Indeed, the growing influence of the Carthaginian Council of Elders on the campaign was reflected by the presence of their representatives in Hannibal's camp. Faced with the necessity of continued appeal both at home and abroad, therefore, Hannibal could not rely solely upon new battlefield tactics to sustain the Carthaginian war effort. The term 'propaganda', with its apparent emphasis on the production and dissemination of a strictly controlled message, often appears out of place in the context of the ancient world, where distance and the lack of effective transport and communication systems worked against such techniques' effective deployment. Nevertheless, despite such limitations, later, retrospective, accounts demonstrate a remarkable consistency in their presentation of the general, and all were based in part upon stories already in circulation at the time of the Second Punic War.

During that period, a body of stories developed around Hannibal which had been produced by individuals who were broadly sympathetic to his cause, or who at least saw him as a viable or necessary bulwark against the growing power of Rome. Although there was no central 'Ministry of Information' directly overseeing this artistic output, the uniformity which one finds in the way that Hannibal and his campaign against Rome were represented by his supporters suggests a studied Carthaginian interest in image and opinion. It was Alexander the Great who had first developed this aspect of ancient warfare, as he traveled across the lands of the East not only with his well-trained armies but also with a coterie of special advisers, writers and intellectuals. Although a number of their accounts of his campaigns were written up after his death, many of the stories with which Alexander was associated, particularly in regard to the divine favor shown to him by his heroic ancestors Hercules and Achilles, were circulated while hostilities were still ongoing, as a way of encouraging friends and potential allies and demoralizing enemies.

For Hannibal, the support of the Greek cities in Magna Graecia was particularly essential if his expedition was to be successful. The long and arduous march to Italy, as well as the fierce resistance that the Romans would undoubtedly put up, meant that reinforcements, supplies and bases would be sorely needed on the peninsula. He thus gathered around himself a small group of trusted confidants, including Sosylus of Sparta, his old teacher, and the Sicilian Greek Silenus of Caleacte, who both 'lived with him as long as fortune allowed'. Polybius, who was generally disparaging towards Hannibal's historians, nevertheless respected Silenus, whose work he may have used as a source for Hannibal's campaigns in Spain. A number of Roman writers certainly rated Silenus, and used his work extensively. Indeed, the famous Roman writer and politician Marcus Tullius Cicero was moved to comment that Silenus was a 'thoroughly reliable authority on Hannibal's life and achievements'.

That Greeks should be such close associates of Hannibal is unsurprising when one considers the long-standing and close contacts between Carthage and the Greek world, particularly in Sicily. From the end of the fourth century BC considerable numbers of Greek mercenaries had fought in the armies of Carthage, and there were close cultural connections. Members of the Carthaginian elite had long been educated in Greek literature, and Hamilcar had ensured that Greek tutors carefully educated Hannibal, to the extent that he had been able to write several books in the language. Hannibal's knowledge of Greek was recognized by later historians as one of his great strengths.

Chapter 6: Man Becomes Myth

Hannibal was presented as the champion of a central-Mediterranean world that had existed before Rome had taken the stage, and whose passing was now increasingly regretted in diverse quarters. One important dissenting voice had been another Sicilian Greek, from Acragas, Philinus, who had written a history of the First Punic War that was sympathetic to Carthage. Indeed, Philinus was well respected by his peers, and his work was used by a number of later scholars, including Polybius. One of Philinus' main themes, which appeared in a number of later Greek writers, was that it was the Romans' acquisitiveness and greed that had led to their assistance to the Mamertines and the subsequent outbreak of hostilities with Carthage, rather than any noble desire to protect the underdog. Indeed, this may have been a commonly held view among Sicilian Greeks, who must have looked with some cynicism towards the intentions of both the Carthaginians and the Romans. Diodorus reports that Hiero, king of Syracuse, said that by coming to the help of the Mamertines 'it would be clear to all of mankind that they [the Romans] were using pity for the endangered as a cloak for their own advantage.'

One identifiable theme in Philinus' history is the focus on those Greeks who had fought on the Carthaginian side in the First Punic War, which might be seen as an implicit rejection of the ethnic divisions propagated by Timaeus. Many western Greeks may now have looked back with a certain nostalgia to the days when it was they who had vied for supremacy of the central Mediterranean with Carthage. Now the cities of Magna Graecia had been firmly under Roman control for over half a century. Moreover, the decades after the end of the first conflict between Carthage and Rome had definitely shown that there was to be no renaissance of Greek Sicily.

The multifaceted symbol of Hercules provided a potent shared symbol not only for the culturally diverse troops who already comprised the Carthaginian army, but also for potential new recruits. The Herculean image attributed to Hannibal by his propagandists may well have created cohesion among the Carthaginian army not only by its diverse appeal, but also by the sense of divine favor that it conveyed. An ancient-Greek military strategist, Onasander, writing 300 years after Hannibal, made the following observation: 'Soldiers are far more courageous when they believe that they are facing dangers with the good will of the gods; for they themselves are watchful, each man, and they look out keenly for omens of sight or sound and an auspicious sacrifice for the whole army encourages even those who have private doubts.'

As Gregory Daly has recently pointed out, 'Hellenistic armies apparently developed their espirit de corps based on the mystique of their leaders who could be seen as having almost "supernatural powers" as they were granted triumphs by the gods.' The claim to divine endorsement was a key element of Hannibal's campaign against the Romans, and certainly played to the expectations of Hannibal's Celtic allies, whose chieftains were often accompanied by bards who eulogized their deeds in song. In the writings of the later Roman historian Cassius Dio, the equation between successful leadership and divine sanction is made explicit. Dio attributes Hannibal's ability to predict future events to the fact that 'he understood divination by the inspection of entrails.' At those critical moments when confidence in their mission had begun to ebb away from his troops, Hannibal seems to have ensured that some evidence of divine favor was presented by which the stocks of Carthaginian self-belief were replenished and the troops were reminded that they were literally following in the footsteps of Hercules and his army.

Indeed, when a late-Roman military writer, Vegetius, mistakenly claimed that Sosylus served as a military tactician under Hannibal, he was only partly wrong. The role that Sosylus and other writers within the general's circle played in propagating Carthaginian propaganda was central to the early success of the campaign. On the eve of the army's departure, Hannibal journeyed to Gades, that first great Phoenician bridgehead in the West and the supposed site of Geryon's home island of Erythia.

There he made solemn vows at the altar of Melqart. It appears that this episode was Silenus' work, and it is surely no coincidence that what has survived from his account is a description of the Heracleium, a sacred spring located in the sanctuary of Melqart. Thus, once more, the extent to which Hercules, along with Hannibal, was the central character in Silenus' narrative is highlighted. For Hannibal himself this visit was far more than a public display of pious devotion, for the rites that he performed in the sacred precinct marked the first steps of a carefully choreographed journey. The Herculean association forced home by Silenus can also be seen in another famous anecdote concerning a supposed dream of the Carthaginian general. Below is the version supplied by Cicero, which is thought to be the most accurate rendition of Silenus' original: The following too is found in the Greek history of Silenus, whom Coelius follows and who gave a most thorough account of Hannibal's career. Hannibal (he says), after taking Saguntum, dreamed that he was being called away by Jupiter into a council of gods; when he arrived, Jupiter ordered him to invade Italy, and gave him one of the assembly as his guide. He had begun the march together with his army, under the guide's leadership; then that guide told him not to look behind him.

He could not carry that through, and borne away by desire, he had turned to look back, and saw a vast monstrous wild beast, intertwined with snakes, destroying all of the trees and shrubs and buildings wherever it went. Staggered, he had asked the god, what such a monstrous thing could be. 'The devastation of

Italy,' answered the god; 'go forward and do not worry about what is happening behind your back.' Although other versions of this episode were adapted by their Roman authors to place Hannibal in a sinister and ultimately flawed light, the original story appears to have hailed from the sympathetic pen of Silenus. The pro-Hannibalic tint of the initial version is indeed confirmed by the hostile reaction of the Roman writer Valerius Maximus, who described it as a 'definite prediction, hateful to any person of Roman blood'. Indeed, the fact that it was so widely reported and discussed would suggest that it had a considerable impact. The main emphasis of the dream is that Hannibal has divine sanction to pursue a war with Rome, a sanction confirmed by the approval of Jupiter/Zeus and his provision of a divine guide (who must surely be Hercules). The beast that Hannibal sees wreaking the 'devastation of Italy' has been variously interpreted, but most plausibly as the Hydra, the many-headed serpent which Hercules was commanded to kill as his second labor. The problem in fulfilling that task, so it proved, was that the beast's heads would spontaneously reappear once severed–a problem eventually overcome by cauterizing the wounds to prevent regrowth.

In Silenus' tale, therefore, as Hannibal is represented by Hercules, so Rome is represented by the Hydra, the self-perpetuating monster which the western hero is called to overcome. Indeed, one of Pyrrhus' advisers had once likened Rome to the Hydra precisely for the city's extraordinary capacity for self-renewal. The original story therefore signified not only the divine sanction and Herculean quality of Hannibal, but also Rome's monstrous nature and destruction of its allies' territory. The message of Silenus' vignettes may therefore have been that the great god/hero of the old Mediterranean world had risen once more and called the faithful to muster, for now the time had come to civilize the barbarous and drive the Roman monster into the sea.

Other scholars have argued that Coelius had deliberately doctored Silenus' tale, omitting an important detail about a terrible storm that appears in the versions given by Livy and Cassius Dio. They contend that Coelius' intention was to change the location of the dream from its original place—as Hannibal's army crossed the Alps—to earlier, just after the final fissure with Rome. This would mean that, in its proper context, the point of the dream was to encourage the Carthaginian army in their efforts to keep moving forward and to master the difficult conditions and terrain that faced them. Both Polybius and Livy acknowledge a Hannibalic propaganda campaign which attempted to surround the Carthaginian general with divine associations. In fact their complaints serve as confirmation of just how successful Hannibal's literary entourage had been in pushing the idea of the expedition as divinely sanctioned. As the stories of how Hannibal had tamed this wild land and its even wilder peoples multiplied, so his claim to be heir to Hercules became ever more sure. Thus Polybius condemned certain anonymous writers because: While introducing Hannibal as a commander of unequalled courage and foresight, they incontestably represent him to us as entirely lacking in prudence, and again being unable to bring their series of fabrications to any conclusion or issue they introduce gods and the sons of gods into the sober history of the facts. By representing the Alps as being so steep and rugged that not only horses and troops accompanied by elephants, but even active men on foot would have difficulty in passing, and at the same time picturing to us the desolation of the country as being such, that unless some god or hero had met Hannibal and showed him the way, his whole army would have gone astray and perished utterly, they unquestionably fall into both the above vices.

Livy, in turn, has a Roman commander exhort his troops before battle against the Carthaginian general to find out 'whether this Hannibal is, as he gives out, the rival of Hercules in his journeys, or whether he has been abandoned by his father to pay tax and tribute and to be the slave of the Roman people'. Indeed, the heavy emphasis that Livy places on the impiety of Hannibal throughout his account of the war is probably connected with the disquiet that the Carthaginian's association with Hercules engendered in Rome. What made Hannibal such a potent threat was not merely his military might, but the challenge that he presented to the previously successful Roman model of territorial conquest and incorporation. The relentless divine associations attributed to the Carthaginian general by his literary entourage represented something far more potent than mere self-indulgence. Hannibal was intent on setting out a clear alternative not only to Roman political hegemony, but also to the Roman mythology by which that hegemony was justified. The Romans' own promotion of the cult of Hercules had provided a much-needed mythical and historical affirmation for the huge territorial gains in Italy and in the old Carthaginian colonial possessions in the central Mediterranean. Hannibal's appropriation of Hercules placed a large question mark over such claims. Hannibal appears to have been determined to wrest from Rome not only the military but also the propagandist initiative.

The Romans found themselves recast by Hannibal's literary entourage in a new and unfamiliar role: as the agents of a tyranny from which the great hero was destined to liberate Italy. Rome, it appeared, was the new Cacus. In attempting to unite the Punic, Greek and Italian communities under the banner of Hercules–Melqart, Hannibal was attempting to drive Rome out of the god/hero's ancient realm. Timaeus had underlined the 'historic' ties that supposedly bound the Romans and the western Greeks against the Carthaginians, but now his heirs embarked on a bold project to dismantle that proposition. From the outset, Hannibal's assault on Rome aimed not only to reduce the city's present formidable power base in the central

Mediterranean, but also to undermine increasingly confident Roman claims to a distinguished past that foretold Rome's emergence as a regional superpower.

Chapter 7: Crossing the Alps

The scale of the undertaking ahead must have struck Hannibal the moment the Hiberus had been traversed. He could possibly have obtained appreciated communications of support from Celtic chiefs in the Alpine regions and the Po valley, to whom he had sent emissaries packed with gifts, but the Spanish native tribes who resided in north-eastern Spain were most certainly not so well pleased towards his appearance. His armies met particularly fierce opposition in the hills of the Pyrenees, resulting in significant losses. So hostile was the reaction of the local peoples that Hannibal was forced to post a force of 10,000 foot soldiers and 1,000 cavalry there in order to hold the mountain passes and secure his rearguard. His army was additionally weakened when 3,000 infantry from the Carpetani, a group that had been recently suppressed, abandoned.

Understanding that they would be additionally more of a liability if they continued to be in his force, Hannibal dispatched away an additional 7,000 men whose dedication was uncertain. Upon traversing the Pyrenees, the state of affairs did not really improve, for the Gallic people who lived in south-western France, fearful of conquest, mustered their fighting men in order to repel the Carthaginian military. It is hardly surprising that many of the peoples who populated the region saw the Carthaginians as becoming considerably more of an immediate threat than the Romans. Full-scale battle was averted only by the distribution of gifts. Adhering to the range of the Mediterranean coast, Hannibal and his army moved through Gaul, and by the conclusion of August 218 they had arrived at the next great natural barrier between them and Italy: the Rhône. This would be Hannibal's biggest obstacle yet. The Rhône was a vast area of water, and on the opposite side waited an army of hostile Volcae tribesmen. In order to counter this, Hannibal transferred his nephew Hanno with a detachment of his Spanish soldiers to cross the river 40 kilometers upstream, with the intention of attacking the Gauls from the rear. When they were in position, they would let Hannibal and the central army know by smoke signal.

The next day, as the main army started to cross the river on a flotilla of small craft and rafts, some of the horses swam across (led by long reins), while others traveled on the boats, saddled and ready to spring into action once they reached the other side. On being attacked by Hanno and his troops, however, the Volcae panicked and fled. The elephants within Hannibal's entourage nevertheless presented another problem. Most ancient writers were of the opinion that elephants were frightened of water and could not swim, and Polybius even repeated a story that some of Hannibal's elephants, panicked by the water, plunged into the river, and crossed to the other side by walking underwater on the riverbed and using their trunks as snorkels. To get their elephants across to the other bank, the Carthaginians came up with an ingenious solution. Huge rafts were constructed covered with a thick layer of earth so that the elephants would be tricked into thinking that they were still on terra firma. To encourage the bulls, two females were led on to the rafts first. Thus the whole squadron crossed safely. The crossing of the Rhône would very much set the tone for the other events which provided the narrative links in the chain of the long march to Italy. Each story had as a common theme both the conquest of seemingly insurmountable natural obstacles and the taming of wild beasts and barbarous peoples. Thus Hannibal's journey to Italy came increasingly to resemble a series of Herculean labors.

Indeed, the strong association between the expedition and the Herculean odyssey may have injected some awkwardness into overtures towards indigenous peoples, for, while the Carthaginian general eagerly sought out their friendship in order to gain access to manpower and supplies, Hannibalic ideology placed a heavy emphasis on the pacification of the land not only as a physical barrier but also in regard to the people who lived there. Hannibal's elephants played a starring role in these adventures, and on the battlefield they would stand for the seemingly unstoppable might of the Carthaginian forces. However, the stories connected with the crossing of the Rhône and, later, of the Alps also played on the essential vulnerability of these giant beasts in unfamiliar territory.

Through being able to control these formidable and mercurial creatures in even the most difficult of circumstances, Hannibal would prove himself equal even to the great Hercules, who had led Geryon's cattle over the same route. Before embarking on his account of Hannibal's epic journey over the Alps, Polybius provided his readership with an impromptu geography lesson. In typically censorious style, the Greek historian voiced his disapproval of those fellow writers who bamboozled their audience with a daunting list of strange names. Whether they liked it or not, those who read the histories of Polybius would know exactly where Hannibal and his armies had been.

In addition, Polybius particularly emphasized the precedents for Hannibal's supposedly unique feat: 'Similarly in what they [other historians] say about the loneliness, and the extreme difficulty and steepness of the road, the falsehood is manifest. For they never took the trouble to learn that the Celts who lived near the Rhône not on one or on two occasions only before Hannibal's arrival but often, and not at any remote date but quite recently, had crossed the Alps with large armies.' According to Polybius, crossing the mighty Alps was an almost mundane exercise, easily within the capabilities of a large Celtic rabble. The feat for which Hannibal was most celebrated thus became a mere cipher for barbarity. Hannibal, rather than being a new Hercules taming the wild Alps, was just one in a long line of barbarian invaders hoping to break into Roman territory. Polybius had felt able to pass such a damning judgment on Hannibal's achievement because he had, according to his own account, actually visited the Alps and painstakingly gathered evidence by talking to the locals, even walking some of the route that Hannibal had taken. The truth, however, was that Polybius' account of his Alpine research trip was really an indication of the gaping distance between himself and his subject. The area known as Cisalpine Gaul and Liguria had been radically transformed by the time that Polybius visited it. The 'locals' whom Polybius grilled were not the Celts who had peopled that region during the time of Hannibal's crossing, but Roman settlers sent there long after the Second Punic War, when the region had at last been militarily subdued by Rome and many of its previous Celtic inhabitants deported.

For the Greek historian wandering around the new farmsteads and settlements of the Roman colonists, the idea that this place had just a few short years ago been a dangerous and hostile environment could be dismissed as alarmist nostalgia. In 218 BC, however, the situation had been very different. The Celtic people who lived in the Alpine regions had long been a thorn in the side of Rome. Commonly known as 'Gauls' in both Latin and Greek texts, they had in 387 BC swept down into central Italy and inflicted the terrible humiliation of occupying Rome. The Po valley, where these tribes lived, was worth fighting for. By the mid third century BC it was the largest parcel of fertile land on the Italian peninsula outside Roman control. If it were captured, new homes and cheap food could be provided for Rome's dispossessed and discontented poor. There were also other, more defensive, strategic considerations that informed Rome's northern-Italian policy. Ancient commentators appear to have been united in their analysis that while

Rome did not control this area 'not only would they [the Romans] never be the masters of Italy but they would not even be safe in Rome itself'. In 225 BC a large force of 50,000 infantry and 20,000 cavalry mainly made up of two Gallic tribes, the Boii and the Insubres, had again marched down the Po valley and had advanced on Etruria. It was only after an emphatic Roman victory over this force in battle that the Roman Senate decided on a systematic plan for conquering the region.

Two new Roman colonies were established on Gallic territory, at Cremona and Placentia, and by 220/219 the Via Flaminia, which connected the region to Rome, was also completed. Now the approach of Hannibal put these hard-fought gains in jeopardy, with the Boii and the Insubres once more in open revolt (no doubt encouraged by the ambassadors whom Hannibal had instructed to foment unrest). The Roman armies sent to subdue the revolt suffered humiliating defeats and were driven from the region, and an attempt to recover the strategically crucial Po valley was also a catastrophic failure, with the Roman forces annihilated. Although the Celts were generally denigrated by Roman and Greek authors for their lack of endurance, tendency to panic and lack of military discipline (as well as their drunkenness), it was also recognized that they could be a very effective fighting force. The intimidating mixture of their wild appearance, blood-curdling war cries and ferocious charges made them a tough proposition, even for a disciplined and experienced Roman army. Their menace to Rome had, however, previously been diluted by their inability to maintain alliances with one another, and in later Greek and Roman historians the perfidy of the Celts became proverbial.

According to one damning assessment, they were 'naturally more or less fickle, cowardly or faithless . . . And the fact that they were no more faithful to the Carthaginians will teach the rest of mankind a lesson never to dare invade Italy.' The potential danger for the Romans was that Hannibal might manage successfully to unite the Celtic tribes under his charismatic command. While Hannibal himself never really trusted the Celts (it was said that he possessed several wigs and other disguises to guard against treachery), many of the alliances he made with them gave him invaluable access to much-needed reinforcements and front-line shock troops. At the same time as Hannibal was approaching the Alps, the Roman consul Publius Cornelius Scipio had landed his army near the port of Massilia, with the intention of attacking Barcid Spain. Scipio might have arrived there much more quickly if he had not been delayed by the rebellion of the Boii and the Insubres, in response to which the Romans were forced to use one of the legions given to him for his new Spanish campaign. Scipio had therefore been obliged to recruit another new legion, and had arrived in southern Gaul three months behind schedule. On landing, he quickly sent out 300 horsemen to ascertain the whereabouts of Hannibal and his forces.

These Roman scouts soon ran into a group of Numidian cavalry who were fulfilling the equivalent role for Hannibal, and, after a skirmish in which the Numidians suffered fairly heavy losses, the Roman cavalry returned to their camp to pass on the location of the Carthaginian army. Scipio quickly set off in hot pursuit. Hannibal initially vacillated between engaging with Scipio's legions and continuing on to Italy, but his mind was finally made up by the arrival in the Carthaginian camp of emissaries from the Boii, who both offered to act as guides across the rugged terrain ahead and promised an alliance.

When Scipio arrived at the site of Hannibal's camp, he found that the Carthaginians had long gone. Instead of rushing after Hannibal in pursuit of glory, however, he returned to northern Italy in order to defend the Po valley. At the same time, he decided to raise fresh troops for this mission and left the greater part of his original force under the command of his brother Gnaeus, with orders to proceed with the original mission of invading the Iberian peninsula. This decision proved crucial, for it effectively ended any chance of Hannibal receiving reinforcements from Spain. Hannibal approached the Alpine region at some speed, hoping to put as much distance as possible between Scipio and himself. For both topographical and propagandist reasons, he must surely have desired to continue on the Herculean way via the river Durance and Mont Genèvre, but Scipio's retreated army now blocked that route. Hannibal's subsequent route is unclear, but it is most likely that he traveled north following the river Rhône. There in the territory of the Allobroges he made valuable allies by adjudicating in a dispute between two royal brothers over who should rule. Aided by guides given by the grateful new ruler, and provided further with supplies, warm clothes and food, he and his troops then set off across the Alps.

By now it was October and winter was fast closing in, and as the Carthaginian army prepared its ascent through the valley of the Arc, probably after marching through the Isère valley, it lost its friendly guides, who returned home. Despite Polybius' claims to the contrary, the Alps presented possibly the most formidable barrier on the European continent. One later Roman historian described how in the spring season men, animals and wagons slipped and slithered on the melted ice towards precipitous ravines and treacherous chasms. In the winter, conditions were even worse.

Even on the level ground, lines of posts were driven through the snow so that travelers knew where it was safe to tread to escape being swallowed up by the treacherous voids which lurked just under the surface of the snowfall. Ominously, other Allobrogian chiefs, sensing easy pickings to help them through the harsh winter ahead, had started to muster their tribesmen on the high ground, ready for an attack on the vulnerable Carthaginian column below. Now Hannibal showed that he was as skilled in mind games as in armed combat. Finding out from his scouts where the Alpine tribesmen were planning an ambush, he and a group of select men occupied a nearby site while the complacent Allobroges slept in their village. When the tribesmen started to attack his army, Hannibal and his troops rushed down and drove them off, killing many of them. He then stormed the Gallic settlement, and not only freed a number of his men and animals who had been captured the previous day, but also seized the contents of the tribesmen's corn store. A few days later, Gallic chieftains came forward and offered friendship, hostages and guides. Hannibal, suspicious of their motives, accepted their overtures while at the same time preparing for treachery. Two days later, as the Carthaginians traveled through a narrow pass they were ambushed by a strong force of Gauls.

Fortunately Hannibal had prepared for this eventuality by moving his vulnerable baggage train and cavalry to the front of the column, and positioning heavy infantry at the rear where the tribesmen attacked. The tribesmen were eventually repulsed, but nevertheless they continued in small groups to make isolated attacks on the column, rolling boulders down the steep slopes on to the men and animals below. Finally, nine days into their march, the Carthaginians reached the top of the pass.

After waiting two days for stragglers to catch up, Hannibal rallied his exhausted and dispirited troops by showing them the panorama of Italy below and, according to Livy, delivering a spirited exhortation. Such encouragement was sorely needed. It was now late October, and the winter snows had begun to fall. What was more, the descent into Italy was even steeper than the past ascent. The track was precipitous, narrow and slippery, and it was almost impossible for men or beasts to keep on their feet. Eventually the army reached what at first looked like the premature end of their odyssey. In front of them was a steep precipice, which a recent landslide had turned into a vertical drop of some 300 meters. Livy dramatically describes the attempt to bypass it: The result was a horrible struggle, the ice affording no foothold in any case, and least of all on a steep slope. When a man tried by hands or knees to get on his feet again, even those useless supports slipped from under him and let him down; there were no stumps or roots anywhere to afford an attachment to either hand or foot; in short there was nothing for it but to roll and slither on the smooth ice and melting snow. Sometimes the mules' weight would drive their hooves through into the lower layer of old snow; they would fall and, once down, lashing savagely out in their struggles to rise, they would break right through it, so that as often as not they were held as in a vice by a thick layer of hard ice. The situation was now critical, and Hannibal ordered that snow be cleared high up on the ridge so that camp could be pitched. It had been decided that the only way of proceeding down the sheer slope would be by cutting a stepped route through the rock.

The means by which this was achieved became one of the most famous tales in the Hannibalic canon: It was necessary to cut through the rock, a problem that they solved by the ingenious application of heat and moisture; large trees were cut down and logged, and a huge pile of timber was built up; this, with the opportune aid of a strong wind, was set on fire, and when the rock was sufficiently heated the men's rations of sour wine were flung upon it in order to render it friable. They then proceeded to work with picks on the heated rock and opened a sort of zigzag track, to minimize the steep gradient of the descent; they were, therefore, able to get the pack animals and even the elephants down it. Many aspects of this story of course appear fanciful, and it may reasonably be doubted whether the Carthaginians were able to acquire such quantities of wood, let alone to heat rock to a sufficient temperature. Nevertheless, the dissemination of such tales from the Carthaginian camp served a vital agenda. Quite simply, the heroic creation of a new Hannibalic way through impermeable Alpine rock was a brilliant piece of propaganda. Through the production of such heroic tales, Hannibal ensured that his name would be indelibly linked with the great mountain chain that he had successfully crossed. Despite Polybius' denigration of this stupendous achievement, it would not be until the reign of the emperor Augustus (31 BC–AD 14) that a Roman would traverse the Alps. Indeed, Hannibal's Alpine adventures would remain a source of wonder for both Greek and Roman writers, producing a vast number of different theories on the actual route that the Carthaginian troops took through the mountains. Even 600 years later the section of the mountains through which Hannibal passed was still called 'the Punic Alps'

Chapter 8: The Die is Cast

The great Alpine trial was now at an ending, and the plains of northern Italy stretched out before the Carthaginian army. Yet heroic grandeur and the element of shock had arrived at an extreme price. The journey that had taken the Carthaginian army from Spain to northern Italy had been epic in every sense, including the scale of human loss. Hannibal had departed the Iberian peninsula alongside 50,000 foot infantry and 9,000 horse cavalry, but by the point he had gotten to the river Rhône these numbers had dwindled to 38,000 and 8,000 respectively. The crossing of the Alps had cut those figures down to just 20,000 infantry and 6,000 cavalry. Regardless of whether or not the initial size of the Carthaginian armed force was overstated, the collateral damage of Hannibal's Alpine crossing was as spectacular as his feats of valor. Like many armies on unbelievable journeys, however, the majority of soldiers were lost not to enemy steel, the icy cold, starvation or, in this instance, even the steep precipices of the Alpine peaks. Many, confronted by significant hardship, exertion and danger, had simply deserted.

But, for all the losses, there could no doubt that this daring enterprise had been a glittering success. After all, new troops could now be recruited and supplies gathered. More importantly, if the Hellenistic world and the Italian city states had not taken the young Carthaginian general seriously before, they certainly would now. Before the battle for Italy began, however, Hannibal engaged in a little housekeeping. The loyalty, or at least the compliance, of the Celts could not be guaranteed by blandishments and expensive gifts alone. An example had to be made so that the price of hostility to the Carthaginian cause could be gauged and understood. Once the Roman armies were successfully engaged, there would be little time to keep the northern Celts in check. The Taurini, a tribe who had attempted to resist the

Carthaginian advance, were picked out as the poor unfortunates who would provide the painful lesson.

Their capital was besieged and soon taken, and its inhabitants–men, women and children–were massacred. Thus a brutal, bloody message which spelled out the consequences of resistance was sent out to the Gallic tribes. However, the massacre also served another purpose, for, as the final act of the great Alpine crossing, the slaughter of the Taurini stood as a further reminder of Hannibal's claim to the lion-skinned mantle of that great hero who had first tamed the wild peoples of this barbarous land. In Rome, the news that Hannibal had successfully crossed the Alps was met with grave alarm. The consul Tiberius Sempronius Longus was recalled from Sicily to assist his colleague Publius Cornelius Scipio, who was now marching towards the river Po in order to confront the Carthaginian army. Before the first confrontation between the two armies, at the river Ticinus, a tributary of the Po, Hannibal, in order to prepare his army psychologically for the hardships that undoubtedly lay ahead, took the unusual step of offering his Gallic prisoners the opportunity of freedom if they emerged victorious from a series of bouts of single combat. Previously he had ensured that these young men had been ill-treated and starved, in order to create the maximum impact when they were led out in front of his assembled troops. To exaggerate further the contrast between the present miserable plight of the captives and the possibilities which both triumph and defeat would offer, Hannibal also brought forth some suits of armor, rich military cloaks and horses as rewards for the victors. All the prisoners clamored to take up Hannibal's offer, for both victory and, through death, defeat offered release from their present servitude.

After the bouts, the Carthaginian troops found themselves pitying those who had not been chosen for combat but remained captive even over those who had been killed. Polybius gives an account of what happened next: When Hannibal had by this means produced the disposition he desired in the minds of his troops, he rose and told them that he had brought the prisoners before them with the purpose that, clearly seeing in the person of the others what they might themselves have to suffer, they would better understand the present crisis. 'Fortune', he said, 'has brought you to a pass, she has locked you into a similar battlefield, and the prizes and prospects she offers you are the same. For either you must conquer, or die, or fall captive into the hands of your foes. For you the prize of victory is not to possess horses and cloaks, but to be the most envied of mankind, masters of all the wealth of Rome. The prize of death on the battlefield is to depart from life in the heat of the fight, struggling until your last breath for the noblest of objects and without having learned to know suffering. But what awaits those of you who are vanquished and for the love of life wish to flee, or who preserve their lives by any other means, is to have every evil and every misfortune as their fate. There is not one of you so dim and unreflecting as to hope to reach his home by flight, when he remembers the length of the road he traversed from his native land, the numbers of the enemies that lie between, and the size of the rivers he crossed. I beseech you, therefore, cut off as you are entirely from any such hope, to take the same view of your own situation that you have just expressed regarding that of others. For as you all considered both the victor and the dead fortunate and pitied the survivors, so now should you think about yourselves and go all of you to battle resolved to conquer if you can, and, if this be impossible, to die. And I implore you not to let the hope of living after defeat enter your minds at all. If you reason and decide as I urge upon you, it is clear that victory and safety will follow; for none ever who either by necessity or choice decided on such a course have been deceived in their hope of putting their enemies to flight. And when the enemy has the opposite hope, as is now the case with the Romans, most of them being sure of finding safety in flight as their homes are near at hand, it is evident that the courage of those who despair of safety will carry all before them.'

Later, just before the battle, Hannibal called his men together for some final words of encouragement. He promised land, money, Carthaginian citizenship and freedom to the massed ranks of his troops if victorious. Then, as a sign of the inviolability of his oath, Hannibal picked up a lamb in one hand and a stone in the other and sent up a prayer to Baal Hammon and the other gods that they should kill him if he broke his word. He then dashed the animal's brains out. The battle itself ended in a complete rout of the Roman forces. Hannibal, realizing the great advantage that he possessed in both numbers and quality of cavalry, had recalled the Numidian prince Maharbal and his squadron of 500 horsemen from a raiding mission. Perhaps overconfident in the ability of his javelin-throwers to keep the Carthaginian cavalry at bay, Scipio had placed them in front with his own horse in reserve, but the Roman cavalry were called quickly into action when the javelin-throwers retreated behind them. Eventually a party of Hannibal's Numidian horse managed to outflank the Roman cavalry, and rode down the foot soldiers behind, who panicked and fled. The Roman horse soon followed. Matters were made worse for the Romans by the fact that Scipio was badly wounded, and Livy reports that the general's 17-year-old son Publius, fighting in his first battle, saved the life of his father, although the historian also alludes to an alternative version of the events, in which Scipio suffered the indignity of being rescued by a Ligurian slave. In pain, and lacking confidence in his inexperienced troops, Scipio immediately ordered a Roman withdrawal from the area.

Although the Romans managed to delay the Carthaginians' advance by destroying their pontoon over the river, Hannibal quickly found a suitable place on the Po for his engineers to build another bridge. Meanwhile Scipio, feeling increasingly insecure after the desertion of a large contingent of Gallic troops and the betrayal of the town of Clastidium by its Italian commander, withdrew once more, across the river Trebia, and set up camp on high ground overlooking the east bank, where he waited for reinforcements. Eventually, in mid-December 218, Sempronius Longus arrived with fresh troops. Conscious that his term of office was drawing to a close, and with it the chance of a glorious triumph, Longus was impatient to engage the Carthaginian army in open battle, especially as his own troops appeared to have come off best in a number of minor skirmishes. In fact Hannibal had merely withdrawn his troops near the Trebia, preferring to conserve his military strength for an encounter of his own choosing. The strategy had worked, because Longus, buoyed by these meaningless victories, was ready to commit his forces to a major confrontation. Scipio attempted to get his consular colleague to reconsider, arguing that their raw troops needed more training over the winter months, and that a period of inactivity would ensure that the notoriously fickle Gauls would start to question their new-found allegiance to Hannibal. Longus, however, was not to be deterred, and Hannibal did everything in his power to encourage a Roman attack. After boosting Longus' self-confidence, Hannibal now set the trap. Selecting an area between the two camps where plants and undergrowth covered the steep sides of a riverbank, he organized an ambush party of 1,000 horse cavalry and an equal number on foot under the command of his brother Mago. The next day at dawn he sent his Numidian cavalry across the Trebia, where they proceeded to provoke the Romans by hurling javelins and abuse at their camp. Predictably, Longus ordered his troops to pursue them.

Although the whole Roman force forded the river and drew up into their battle lines in good order, the troops were cold, wet and hungry after being mobilized before they had breakfasted. In contrast, the Carthaginian troops had been well prepared and fed. Both sides appear to have had around 40,000 men each, and, although the heavily armed foot soldiers in the center were evenly matched, once again Hannibal's superior and more numerous cavalry easily bested their Roman counterparts, leaving the flanks of the Roman infantry exposed to attack. It was then that Mago's small force launched its ambush on the rear of the Roman infantry. Around 10,000 Roman soldiers managed to fight their way out and make it to the nearby town of Placentia, but many others were killed. Longus escaped and subsequently tried to convince his fellow citizens that the defeat had occurred only because of the extreme weather conditions. However, few if any appear to have believed him. Meanwhile, it took Hannibal little time to persuade the Italian cities to desert the Romans. The Roman and Italian prisoners of war were treated in quite different ways: the former were put on starvation rations; the latter consular colleague to reconsider, arguing that their raw troops needed more training over the winter months, and that a period of inactivity would ensure that the notoriously fickle Gauls would start to question their new-found allegiance to Hannibal. Longus, however, was not to be deterred, and Hannibal did everything in his power to encourage a Roman attack. After boosting Longus' self-confidence, Hannibal now set the trap. Selecting an area between the two camps where plants and undergrowth covered the steep sides of a riverbank, he organized an ambush party of 1,000 horse cavalry and an equal number on foot under the command of his brother Mago. The next day at dawn he sent his Numidian cavalry across the Trebia, where they proceeded to provoke the Romans by hurling javelins and abuse at their camp. Predictably, Longus ordered his troops to pursue them.

Although the whole Roman force forded the river and drew up into their battle lines in good order, the troops were cold, wet and hungry after being mobilized before they had breakfasted. In contrast, the Carthaginian troops had been well prepared and fed. Both sides appear to have had around 40,000 men each, and, although the heavily armed foot soldiers in the center were evenly matched, once again Hannibal's superior and more numerous cavalry easily bested their Roman counterparts, leaving the flanks of the Roman infantry exposed to attack. It was then that Mago's small force launched its ambush on the rear of the Roman infantry. Around 10,000 Roman soldiers managed to fight their way out and make it to the nearby town of Placentia, but many others were killed. Longus escaped and subsequently tried to convince his fellow citizens that the defeat had occurred only because of the extreme weather conditions. However, few if any appear to have believed him. Meanwhile, it took Hannibal little time to persuade the Italian cities to desert the Romans. The Roman and Italian prisoners of war were treated in quite different ways: the former were put on starvation rations; the latter were treated well and eventually sent home. Before they left, Hannibal addressed them and said that 'he had not come to make war on them, but on the Romans for their sakes; and therefore if they were wise they should embrace his friendship, for he had come first of all to re-establish the liberty of the peoples of Italy and also to help them to recover the cities and territories of which the Romans had deprived them.' The harsh winter of 218/217 granted the Romans some respite, for Hannibal lost a large number of men and horses to the bitter cold, as well as all but one of his elephants. After wintering in Bologna, the Carthaginians moved south and crossed the Apennines into Etruria. They suffered terribly as they spent four days and three nights tramping through terrain so marshy that it was impossible to set up camp. Hannibal, who rode on top of the one remaining elephant, was afflicted by opthalmia, which led eventually to blindness in one eye. In recognition of the threat that they now faced, the Romans had mobilized over 100,000 fighting men.

Concerned that the Carthaginians might launch attacks on Rome's new central-Mediterranean empire, it was decided to send two legions to defend Sicily and another to Sardinia. Two further legions were charged with the defense of Rome itself. The four legions, now under the split command of the two new consuls, Gaius Flaminius Nepos and Gnaeus Servilius Geminus, were reinforced to make up their losses to Hannibal in the previous year. Flaminius was an impetuous and arrogant man, whom Hannibal immediately tried to goad into rash action by ravaging the agriculturally rich Chianti region where Flaminius and his army were stationed. He consequently managed to lure Flaminius and his army into the Borghetto pass, where on the shore of Lake Trasimene an ambush had been set. The mist of the early morning of June 21, 217 made it visibility poor, and the Romans did not see the danger until it was too late.

Chaos ensued, and over 15,000 Roman troops were cut down, including Flaminius himself. Some retreated into the waters of the lake, where they drowned in their heavy armor, and 6,000 troops who had survived surrendered when they realized the hopelessness of their situation. In his treatment of them, Hannibal continued his policy of distinguishing between Roman and Italian prisoners, for the latter were sent home without ransom, while the former languished in captivity. The Carthaginian general also had the superior Roman heavy armor and weapons collected up and redistributed to his own Libyan infantry. A few days later the other consul, Geminus, lost virtually all his cavalry as another surprise attack rendered his force virtually worthless.

According to Livy, the news that arrived in Rome after the Carthaginian victory told not only of military defeat, but also of strange and ominous portents in central Italy. Particularly notable are reports that blood had appeared in the sacred spring of Hercules at Caere, an apparent indication of the success with which

Hannibal had associated himself with the hero. The Roman reaction, which consisted in offering up prayers at the shrine, certainly suggests an attempt to win Hercules back to the Roman cause. The battle for supremacy was thus being fought on both the temporal and the celestial plane. Hannibal, recognizing the poor physical shape that his troops and animals were now in, decided to recuperate on the more clement Adriatic coast.

According to Polybius, the Carthaginians had by that time captured so much booty that they had grave difficulty transporting it to their new base. After two years away from the sea, Hannibal now had the opportunity to send a message back to Carthage to inform the Council of his victories. The news was met with great celebration in North Africa, and Carthage sent back a message promising support for the campaign both in Italy and in Spain. In contrast, the mood in Rome was one of panic, as news of this latest and most terrible defeat trickled in with the survivors. The populace had thronged around the Forum Romanum and the Senate House, waiting for confirmation from the magistrates. On this occasion the disaster was such that no positive spin could be put on it. One of the praetors climbed on to the speaker's rostrum and simply said, 'Pugna magna victi sumus'–'We have been defeated in a great battle.' With one consul dead and the other unable to return, the Romans decided to compromise Republican ideology and appoint a dictator, a temporary autocrat allowed by the constitution only in times of intense crisis. The people chose the vastly experienced Quintus Fabius Maximus, twice consul and once censor, with Marcus Minucius Felix to assist him as Master of the Horse.

Chapter 9: The Retreat of Rome

Fabius, learning from the mistakes of his predecessors, took a completely unique approach to the war against the Carthaginians. Immediately after recruiting two new legions and taking over the two which had been formerly commanded by Geminus, Fabius marched to Apulia, where he resisted Hannibal's attempts to rush him into unrestricted conflict. The Grecian biographer Plutarch provides an obvious overview of these new tactics: He [Fabius] did not really plan to fight out the issue with him [Hannibal], but wished, possessing quite a bit of time, money and men, to wear out and progressively deplete his culminating strength, his meager resources, and his limited military. Therefore, continuously erecting his camp in cragged regions so as to seem to be out of range of the enemy's horse cavalry, he hung menacingly above them all. If they sat still, he too held quiet; but if they relocated, he would descend down from the elevations and show himself just far enough apart to prevent being compelled to battle against his desire, and yet close enough to make his exact delays inspire the adversary with the fear that he was going to give battle at last. Hannibal, appreciating the cleverness of Fabius' strategies, did all in his power to draw his forces out into straightforward battle by provocations such as the ravaging of the fertile areas of Benvento and Campania. The Romans upheld their discipline, nevertheless, tailing the Carthaginian army and picking off raiding parties when they encountered the opportunity.

Even while effective, Fabius' strategies were very unpopular both in his own camp and on the streets of Rome. Long after his death, the Romans would come to be grateful for their cunctator ('delayer'–as Fabius' posthumous epithet would be), but at the instant generations of effective hostile action had enforced the popular perception that such methods were simply un-Roman. Hannibal himself further stoked up the pressure level by sparing the Roman general's own property while burning the majority of the land around it, thus attaching substance to a rumor that Fabius had been secretly bargaining together with him. Eventually, however, it appeared as if Fabius' unpopular method had paid off.

In the autumn of 217 an ever more aggressive Hannibal carried out a terrible mistake that placed his army at the mercy of the Romans. He [Hannibal] desired to draw his forces off some extended distance beyond Fabius, and take up plains affording pasturage. He therefore directed his indigenous guides to conduct him, immediately after the evening dinner, into the district of Casinum. However they did not hear the name correctly, owing to his foreign manner of pronouncing it, and quickly rushed his forces to the edge of Campania, into the urban area and region of Casilinum, through the midst of which flows a separating river, called Vulturnus near the Romans. The region is normally encompassed by mountain ranges, but a narrow gorge opens out towards the sea, in the vicinity of which it becomes marshy, from the runoff of the river, includes high sand-heaps, and terminates in a beach where there is no anchorage as a result of the dashing waves. At the same time Hannibal was climbing down into this valley, Fabius, benefiting from his acquaintance with the approaches, marched around him, and blocked up the narrow exit with a detachment of 4,000 heavy infantry.

The rest of his army he posted to advantage on the remaining heights, while with the lightest and readiest of his troops he fell upon the enemy's rearguard, threw their whole army into confusion, and slew about 800 of them. Hannibal now perceived the mistake in his position, and its peril, and crucified the native guides who were responsible for it. He wished to make a retreat, but despaired of dislodging his enemies by direct attack from the passes of which they were masters. All his men, moreover, were disheartened and fearful, thinking that they were surrounded on all sides by difficulties from which there was no escape. Hannibal may have blamed his local guides, but it was Fabius' dogged determination that had allowed the Roman general to capitalize on this error. Hannibal, however, proved himself equal to the challenge. Learning of the Roman ambush prepared for his army, he waited until nightfall and then tied burning brands to the horns of 2,000 captured cattle. The cattle were then driven up to the high ground where the Roman troops were stationed. In the dark, the Romans, thinking that they were under attack, panicked and fled, allowing Hannibal and his army to pass through unimpeded.

This embarrassing incident led to further scorn and derision being heaped on the unfortunate Fabius, though the Carthaginian escape from this seemingly hopeless situation merely highlighted Hannibal's genius rather than the shortcomings of Fabius' tactics. In Rome, a sizable faction had now decided that the only way of defeating Hannibal was to grant the more aggressive Minucius Felix equal powers to those of Fabius. Despite resistance from Fabius and his supporters in the Senate, the motion was passed, and the Roman forces were thus effectively split between the two commanders. In the wake of his new appointment, Felix immediately attempted to establish his Herculean credentials by dedicating an altar to the hero. Within the context of the Hannibalic campaign, that dedication served to reinforce Roman claims to the Herculean legend, but it perhaps also represented a challenge by Felix to Fabius' own claim to direct Herculean ancestry.

The battle for Hercules thus now engaged competing generals both between and within the two warring states. Fabius, indeed, had been the first Roman general to understand the importance of countering the Carthaginian propaganda onslaught. He had Roman priests consult the Sibylline books, a collection of oracular utterances, to find out how the Romans might regain the favor of the gods, and the priests returned with three recommendations: first, the Romans should publicly renew their vows to Mars, the god of war; second, Fabius should dedicate a temple to the goddess Venus Erycina, a Sicilian goddess, and another to the divine quality of Mens, 'Composure' or 'Resolution'; finally, the Romans should make the pledge of the 'sacred spring', an ancient rite whereby the entire produce of the next spring was promised to the deity of the spring if victory was achieved within a certain time. The foundation of a new temple to Venus Erycina on the Capitol, completed in 215, is immediately notable for its links with the Trojan prince Aeneas, represented in Roman myth as the son of Venus, and by this period widely accepted as the forefather of Romulus and Remus. It was thought that Aeneas had married the daughter of Latinus, the eponymous king of Latium, and that upon the latter's death he had ruled over the Latins and his own Trojan settlers. By the time of the Second Punic War, the Aeneas story had become a keystone in the ideological edifice that legitimized Roman domination of Italy, for it located the origins of that domination within a consensual agreement of the shared, mythological past. The interest for the Romans in 217, however, was not simply in a cult of Venus, but more specifically in a cult of Venus Erycina. That cult was a relatively recent invention, created after the capture of Sicilian Eryx from the Carthaginians in 248.

Although the outer town had soon been retaken by Hamilcar Barca, Hannibal's father, the Roman defenders had withstood several furious assaults and retained the citadel and the sanctuary within. The cult was thus an important symbol of successful Roman resistance against a Carthaginian, and more specifically Barcid, enemy, and its introduction into Rome provided the city with a focal point for resistance to the new Barcid onslaught. At the same time, the city of Eryx had long been sacred to the Punic goddess Astarte and the Greek goddess Aphrodite. The re-branding of the city's patron deity as Aphrodite/Astarte's Roman equivalent Venus therefore represented an attempt not only to 'Romanize' the cult, but simultaneously to integrate Sicily within the Roman foundational myth associated with Aeneas. Conveniently, the indigenous Elymians, whose capital Eryx was, also claimed a Trojan ancestry, and their city of Segesta (as we have seen) had previously appealed to Rome for intervention precisely on the basis of that shared history.

The Roman promotion of the multifaceted cult of Venus Erycina thus emphasized resistance to the Carthaginians while simultaneously incorporating the contested island of Sicily within a Roman vision of history. Eryx and its goddess were now as much disputed as Hercules. His biographer Plutarch portrayed Fabius' activities on this front as having been driven solely by pragmatism rather than superstition: 'By thus fixing the thoughts of the people upon their relations with heaven, Fabius made them more cheerful regarding the future. But he himself put all his hopes of victory in himself, believing that heaven bestowed success by reason of wisdom and courage, and turned his attentions to Hannibal.' However, there can be little doubt that Fabius' religious activities were informed by a recognition that there was a growing concern among the citizens of Rome that the gods were turning against them. It was as if Hannibal had now turned that most Roman of psychological weapons, the evocatio, the ritual through which the gods of Rome's enemies were enticed into defection, against its originators. Later, Livy described the damaging effect that Hannibal's campaign had had on the collective psychology of the Roman people: The longer the war continued, and the more men's minds as well as their fortunes were affected by the alternations of success and failure, so much the more did the citizens become the victims of superstitions, and those for the most part foreign ones.

It seemed as though either the characters of men or the nature of the gods had undergone a sudden change. The Roman ritual was growing into disuse not only in secret and in private houses; even in public places, in the Forum and the Capitol, crowds of women were to be seen who were offering neither sacrifices nor prayers in accordance with ancient usage. Unauthorized sacrificers and diviners had got possession of men's minds, and the numbers of their dupes were swelled by the crowds of country people whom poverty or fear had driven into the city, and whose fields had lain untilled owing to the length of the war or had been desolated by the enemy. These impostors found their profit in trading upon the ignorance of others, and they practiced their calling with as much effrontery as if they had been duly authorized by the state. When eventually the Roman Senate was moved to act in this matter by moving these charlatans and their followers out of the Forum Romanum, a riot almost ensued. This new sense of insecurity also explains the willingness with which the Romans carried out the priests' final recommendation to Fabius: the pledge of a 'sacred spring'. This was one of the oldest and most original elements of Roman religion, and its prescription was clearly no coincidence at a time when those aspects of Roman cultural identity which were shared or contested with other Mediterranean peoples were being so effectively re-framed by Rome's enemies. The 'sacred spring', by contrast, was undisputed a Roman religious rite.

Chapter 10: The Battle of Cannae

Over the following campaign year of 216, the Romans were resolved finally to destroy Hannibal. A monumental army of 87,000 troops was mustered—a quantity that dwarfed the Carthaginian force of around 50,000. The effectiveness of this impressive mobilization was, nevertheless, immediately undermined as a result of the election of two consuls who could not provide the unity that Rome so gravely required, for the two individuals, Gaius Terentius Varro and Lucius Aemilius Paullus, possessed significantly diverging views on exactly how the war against Hannibal should really be waged. Even though Paullus preferred the existing Fabian approach of surrounding Hannibal in his winter quarters and starving him out, Varro was resolved to defeat the Carthaginian general in open battle. Even worse, as both consuls went on campaign, each commanded the army on alternating days. By the end of July, the Roman army had tracked the Carthaginians all the way down to the tiny Apulian town of Cannae, and set up camp around 16 kilometers away. About the first of August, after a series of skirmishes, Hannibal marched his troops northbound across the river Aufidus, set up camp, and subsequently offered the Romans wide-open combat. Paullus, who was in command that day, pointedly refused to acknowledge the challenge, much to the consternation of his associate.

The next day, with Varro in command, the Roman army left its main camp on the north bank of the river and crossed to the south, where it drew up in battle formation facing south, with the river to the west. The previous year's consuls, Servilius Geminus and Atilius Regulus (who had replaced the dead Flaminius Nepos), commanded the heavy infantry in the center, and Paullus led the right wing, where the cavalry and two legions of infantry were situated. Varro himself took command of the left wing, made up of 20,000 infantry and some cavalry. Hannibal took time to study carefully the Roman battle line before making a move. Although greatly outnumbered in terms of heavy infantry, he noticed that the Roman infantry in the center were closely packed together, and would therefore find it difficult to maneuver. After crossing the river with his army, he set up a highly unorthodox but tactically brilliant formation. In the center he placed a series of Celtic and Spanish infantry companies in a shallow-stepped line, and at the end of each line he placed his elite heavily armored Libyan foot soldiers, thus leaving a deliberately weakened center, which he was personally to command with his brother Mago. On both right and left wings he placed his cavalry, under the respective commands of his nephew Hanno and the general Hasdrubal. The Roman infantry not only had the sun in their eyes, but also the wind blew up great clouds of dust into their faces. When battle started, however, they predictably quickly drove back the Spanish and Celtic foot soldiers, and consequently surged forward into the vacuum at the center of the Carthaginian formation. Without a moment's pause they followed up their broken and hastily retreating foe till they took to headlong flight.

Cutting their way through the mass of fugitives, who offered no resistance, they penetrated as far as the Africans who were stationed on both wings, somewhat further back than the Celts and Spaniards who had formed the advanced center. As the latter fell back the whole front became level, and as they continued to give ground it became concave and crescent-shaped, the Africans at either end forming the horns. As the Romans rushed on incautiously between them, they were encircled by the two wings, which extended and closed round them in the rear. On this, the Romans, who had fought one battle to no purpose, left the Celts and Spaniards, whose rear they had been slaughtering, and commenced a fresh struggle with the Africans. The contest was a very one-sided one, for not only were they hemmed in on all sides, but wearied with the previous fighting they were meeting fresh and vigorous opponents. At the same time, the Carthaginian cavalry on the right wing, which had routed the Roman left, now attacked the rear of the Roman right wing, which was thus effectively surrounded. After defeating this force, the combined Carthaginian cavalry then attacked the beleaguered Roman infantry from behind. The Romans were now surrounded, and a bloody slaughter quickly ensued. Paullus, who had been seriously wounded by a sling shot, tried to rally his troops, but his courageous efforts would prove to be in vain. After a while he became too weak to manage his horse, so his cavalry escort dismounted to fight on foot. Although offered the chance to escape on the horse of a fleeing cavalry officer, he refused to leave his men and was eventually killed. Cannae was Rome's greatest military disaster. It is estimated that 70,000 Roman soldiers were killed and another 10,000 captured.

Livy has left us with a ghastly description of the immediate aftermath: The next day, as soon as it grew light, they set about gathering the spoils on the field and viewing the carnage, which was a ghastly sight even for an enemy. There all those thousands of Romans were lying, infantry and cavalry indiscriminately as chance had brought them together in the battle or the flight. Some covered with blood raised themselves from among the dead around them, tortured by their wounds, which were nipped by the cold of the morning, and were promptly put an end to by the enemy. Some they found lying with their thighs and knees gashed but still alive; these bared their throats and necks and drained what blood they still had left. Some were discovered with their heads buried in the earth; they had evidently suffocated themselves by making holes in the ground and heaping the soil over their faces. What attracted the attention of all was a Numidian who was dragged alive from under a dead Roman lying across him; his ears and nose were torn, for the Roman with hands too powerless to grasp his weapon had, in his mad rage, torn his enemy with his teeth, and while doing so expired. Twenty-nine senior Roman commanders and eighty of senatorial rank had lost their lives. Varro, however, the architect of the disaster, somehow escaped with his life. For Hannibal, the path to Rome now lay open. According to Livy, Maharbal, the leader of the Numidian cavalry, urged that the army press on to the city while it had the opportunity: 'That you may know,' he said to Hannibal, 'what has been gained by this battle I prophesy that in five days you will be feasting as victor in the Capitol. Follow me; I will go in advance with the cavalry; they will know that you are come before they know that you are coming.' To Hannibal the victory seemed too great and too joyous for him to realize all at once. He told Maharbal that he commended his zeal, but he needed time to think out his plans. Maharbal replied: 'The gods have not given all their gifts to one man. You know how to win victory, Hannibal, but you do not how to use it.' For Livy, Hannibal's delay was in fact to save Rome from destruction, but in reality the Carthaginian troops and animals were exhausted, and Rome was still 400 kilometers away and well served with defensive fortifications that had been rebuilt in 378.

Made of stone blocks, the Roman city wall was over 5 miles long and interspersed with towers. Even at its weakest points it was bolstered by earthworks, ramps and ditches. Moreover, the city was defended by two urban legions, smaller groups of marines and other troops, as well as by its inhabitants. The capture of Rome would therefore require a long siege and the deployment of powerful siege engines. In fact the actual taking of Rome does not appear to have been one of Hannibal's key objectives, and he instead sought to continue his policy of marginalizing the city from its Italian and Latin allies, so that eventually, when isolated, exhausted and demoralized, it would surrender and seek terms. What Hannibal thus sought was a peace in which Carthage could dictate terms, just as Rome had done in the aftermath of the First Punic War. Towards that end, ten representatives were selected from among the Roman prisoners and were dispatched to Rome to make arrangements for the ransoming of the 8,000 Roman citizens that Hannibal was holding. Before they were released, they all had to swear an oath to return once their mission had been accomplished.

The ransoming of prisoners was a common feature of contemporary warfare, and was often the first stage on the road to a negotiated peace settlement. The Roman response must therefore have shocked Hannibal, for the Senate refused to see the captured Romans, and a decree was passed which forbade the state or private individuals from paying ransoms. Rome had publicly announced its intention to struggle until the bitter end. Hannibal now had little option but to dispose of the prisoners, for they were a dangerous drain on his already stretched resources. Some were executed, and the majority sold into slavery. What sort of terms might Hannibal have sought from Rome? According to Livy, Hannibal claimed in an address to the assembled Roman captives that he did not seek the destruction of their city: 'All he was fighting for was his country's honor as a sovereign power. His fathers had yielded to Roman courage; his one object now was that the Romans should yield to his good fortune and courage.' This is perhaps an accurate assessment of Hannibal's intentions in the aftermath of Cannae. In terms of military and propagandist strategy, the campaign had been a brilliant success. The Roman claims to martial supremacy and to a historical right to rule the Italian peninsula, two of the most important ideological foundations on which Rome's continued expansion had been built, had been utterly undermined.

Indeed, the military campaign had been so extraordinarily successful that it is unlikely that even Hannibal's most optimistic advisers would have envisaged the speed of the Carthaginian success. Hannibal's limited objective at this point is thus perhaps easy to appreciate: not the destruction of Rome itself, but rather its relegation to nothing more than a central Italian power, with the Italian cities liberated and Sardinia and Punic Sicily reclaimed for Carthage. Directly after his greatest military triumph, however, Hannibal had already made his first serious miscalculation, for he assumed that Rome could be forced to negotiate. Hannibal's hybrid education under Sosylus and other Greek tutors might have well prepared him for the intricacies of Hellenistic statecraft, but the contemporary situation now highlighted just how far removed those tutors were from the brutal real politic of the age.

Two centuries later, the triumph of Roman obduracy was an incontrovertible fact around which the Greek intelligentsia would construct their own version of how the Roman state had come to rule the world. In the final decades of the third century BC, however, the Mediterranean world was only slowly beginning to discover the realities of Roman determination.

For Rome, the Italian peninsula was not merely a piece of conquered territory that could be traded or bartered as political circumstance dictated. It would have been a brave politician who suggested that Rome compromise with its enemies or retreat from the hard-won Italian dominions. The Roman senators whom Hannibal faced had been raised on stories that dwelt extensively on their forebears' obstinate refusal to negotiate with the enemy, even in the most desperate of circumstances. That some of these tales concerned examples of heroic Roman grit within living memory, such as Appius Claudius Caecus' refusal to parley with the all-conquering Pyrrhus in 280 BC, only added to their potency. In a society where elite self-representation was so closely associated with mos maiorum, the ways of one's ancestors, to give up the land won by the blood of one's forebears was unthinkable.

During the long years of conflict, Carthage had brought Rome to the brink of disaster on more than one occasion. Upon each instance, however, final victory had been snatched from the Carthaginians' grasp by an enemy who would simply not countenance defeat. The Barcid conquest of the Iberian peninsula had in many respects been an excellent preparation for Hannibal's later confrontation with Rome. Twenty years of almost continuous military campaigning against determined and skilled opposition had turned Hannibal into an excellent general, and honed the Carthaginian army into a superb fighting force. However, in his moment of triumph, Hannibal's poor understanding of the Romans' obdurate mentality now stood in stark contrast to his fine appreciation of their military strengths and weaknesses. Expansion into Spain had helped both to alleviate previous Carthaginian defeats and to compensate for lost territory, but at the same time it had robbed the Carthaginian generals of vital military experience against Rome. If Hannibal had gained such experience, he might not have let the wounded Roman beast escape.

Chapter 11: Pyrrhus of Epirus

It was said that when Hannibal was asked whom he considered to be the greatest commander that had ever lived, he put only Alexander the Great above Pyrrhus, king of Epirus. His explanation was that not only had Pyrrhus been a master military tactician, but 'He possessed, too, the art of winning popularity, to such an extent that the nations of Italy preferred the rule of a foreign king to that of the Roman people who had so long held the foremost place in that country.'

Hannibal's wooing of the Greeks of southern Italy placed him very much within the Pyrrhic tradition. As well as offering obvious strategic advantages (through its relative proximity to North Africa and thus also to potential Carthaginian reinforcements), Greek southern Italy must surely have held great cultural allure for one carefully educated in

Hellenistic mores but hitherto consigned to the 'barbarous' fringes of the Greek world. Yet if Hannibal had spent a little longer studying the history of Pyrrhus' Italian escapade, he might better have understood the difficulties which swiftly arose between the cities of Magna Graecia and the Epirote interloper. Pyrrhus was not the first Hellenistic adventurer to have found that the warm welcome extended to him on his arrival in southern Italy had quickly evaporated. In 334 BC the citizens of Tarentum had appealed to Alexander, king of Epirus, uncle of Alexander the Great, to protect them from the unwelcome attentions of local Italian tribesmen, but it had soon become clear that Alexander himself was a greater threat to Tarentine autonomy than those he had been summoned to fight, and Tarentum was saved from Epirote subjugation only by the king's untimely death. The southern Italian cities had also hailed Pyrrhus as a great defender in their fight against Rome, but relations had again quickly soured.

After two dazzling victories against the Roman army, Pyrrhus decided that he wanted to be more than a mere hired hand, and tried secretly to negotiate a deal with the Romans which proposed that Italy be split between them, with him as ruler of Magna Graecia. The Romans, understanding the immense strategic importance of the region, and perhaps sensing that the danger presented by this brilliant but fickle general would fade away, firmly declined his offer. As Peter Green has observed, 'What the locals wanted was a professional general who stuck to his commission; what they got, as with Alexander of Epirus, was an ambitious conquistador, and, worse, this time one who proved no match for the opposition.' After the previous experience of self-proclaimed Hellenistic 'saviors' in the guise of a new Hercules, it was hardly surprising that the cities of Magna Graecia did not immediately flock to Hannibal's banner. By the end of 216, however, an opportunity to extend Hannibal's influence in southern Italy suddenly presented itself. The wealthy Campanian city of Capua had long been a key Roman ally in the region, and enjoyed the various rights of Roman citizenship as well as the privilege of maintaining its own magistrates. Indeed, many of its elite had close ties with the Roman Senate, often through intermarriage, and a considerable number of the city's young men were serving in the Roman army. With Hannibal now ensconced further north, however, it appears that a number of the ruling elite considered defecting to the Carthaginian cause. Several considerations seem to have influenced their decision. First, worries about the security of the city and its prosperous agricultural hinterland must surely have increased with the news of the disaster at Cannae, and no doubt been further exacerbated by the return home of the Italian prisoners released by Hannibal to spread the news of the Carthaginians' triumph over Rome and generosity to the Italians.

Second, there was resentment at the burdens and obligations that an alliance with

Rome brought, including the commitment to supply troops for the Roman army, the payment of tribute, and the presence of Roman military officials in the city. Finally, and perhaps most importantly, sections of the Capuan elite appear to have envisioned the restoration both of their previous hegemony over Campania and of lands conceded to the Romans. The final break came when a Capuan delegation to Rome voiced their concerns about the deployment of 300 of their well-born youths to the Roman army in Sicily. The Roman consul Varro treated their complaint dismissively, and then warned them that they were now effectively on their own, because of a lack of Roman men and resources to protect them. The pro-Carthaginian members of the Capuan delegation then had little trouble persuading their colleagues to approach Hannibal, and an agreement to hand the city over to him was swiftly reached. In exchange for their support, Hannibal agreed that the Capuans would be allowed to keep their own government and laws. In addition, they would not be forced to undergo military service against their will. The Capuans then returned home, and the rebellion began. All the Roman officials and private citizens in the city were seized and confined in a bathhouse, where they subsequently expired owing to the extreme heat. For Hannibal, Capua was a major catch, and he clearly hoped that its defection would prompt other cities swiftly to follow suit. It was probably for that reason that the Carthaginian general was so generous towards his new allies. According to Livy, Hannibal entered Capua in triumph, and in an address to the Capuan Senate made the ambitious promise that the city would soon be the capital of all Italy, with even Rome subordinate to it.

The vast majority of the people and Senate now lent their weight to the Hannibalic cause. While we cannot know the precise basis of the new alliance, only promises as extravagant as those preserved in Livy can have convinced the Capuans to turn against Rome. The dire consequences of defeat must surely have been recognized. A few Capuans, however, remained unhappy with the new alliance. At a dinner held in his honor, Hannibal was nearly the victim of an assassination attempt by the son of Pacuvius Calavius, one of the leading citizens and a chief supporter of the rebellion, who was only at the last minute dissuaded from carrying out the murder by his father. Another dissident, Decius Magius, who had strongly opposed the new pact on the basis of the precedent of Pyrrhus, was arrested and brought in chains before Hannibal. When ordered by Hannibal to defend himself, however, the feisty Magius refused to do so, citing the very terms of the treaty agreed between the general and the Capuans, which guaranteed the latter's freedom from outside intervention. To avoid further embarrassment, Magius was dragged to a ship bound for Carthage with his head covered, thus preventing his shouts rousing up his fellow citizens against their new allies. While Hannibal now had a major ally in southern Italy, the alliance had come at some cost. The removal of Roman domination was an immediate motivation for Capua's defection, but broader objectives were the maintenance of the city's political autonomy and the restoration of its traditional authority over the whole of Campania. Indeed, the Capuan desire to be recognized as the dominant city in the region is wonderfully illustrated in the minting of a substantial amount of contemporary local coinage which represents the city as a major, independent power.

While Capua was willing to accept Hannibal as the last great bulwark against the encroaching power of Rome, it was willing to do so strictly on its own terms, and only while the alliance accorded with its own regional ambitions. Hannibal had thus been forced to retreat from his promise of Italian liberation in order to ensure the loyalty of a crucial ally. By publicly addressing the issue of Capuan regional hegemony, furthermore, Hannibal had ensured that other Campanian cities were now unlikely to lend him their support. Indeed, subsequent events such as Capua's takeover of the neighboring city of Cumae, and Hannibal's handing over of the captured city of Casilinum, must only have compounded their fears. Although some smaller allies of Capua did join the revolt, the majority of cities in Campania–such as Nola, Naples, Puteoli and Cumae–did not. As Michael Fronda has recently remarked, 'This pattern suggests that long-standing local intercity bonds and rivalries persisted under the veneer of Roman rule and surfaced when Hannibal suspended the mechanisms of Roman rule that suppressed them.' Once more the dreams of a foreign general were set to founder through the complex array of agendas that made up the political landscape of southern Italy. Some cities were now taken by force, but others–most notably Nola –managed to withstand a number of Carthaginian assaults. Livy explained that Hannibal's troops quickly became soft and ill-disciplined once they were stationed in the comfort of Capua, rather than under canvas in the field. A more credible problem was that, in his anxiety to win over the Capuans, Hannibal had absolved them of any obligation to provide him with troops, which left him with a serious recruitment problem.

Furthermore, those who did enlist had neither the experience nor the skill of his precious core of African, Spanish and Celtic troops. This lack of manpower would be further compounded when his brother Hasdrubal, who had been instructed to leave his base in Spain and take his army to Italy, was in 216 heavily defeated by a Roman army under the joint command of the brothers Gnaeus and Publius Scipio at Hibera near the river Hiberus. Hannibal was now compelled to ask the Carthaginian Council for reinforcements via his brother Mago, whom he had dispatched to North Africa earlier that year. Arriving in the Carthaginian Council, Mago dramatically emptied on to the floor a huge pile of gold rings taken from the thousands of dead Roman cavalry who had fallen at Cannae. He then gave an understandably upbeat account of the previous two years of the war, before concluding with a request for fresh troops, supplies and money. His words had the desired effect, for the vast majority of his audience reacted with jubilation. Indeed, one Barcid supporter could not resist a barbed jibe at their old opponent Hanno, mockingly calling for the one Roman senator in the Carthaginian Council to comment. Hanno, however, was far too experienced a political campaigner to be cowed into silence.

In a measured but caustic response, he examined the fragile foundations on which Hannibal's great victories had been built: 'But even now, what is it that you are rejoicing at? "I have slain the armies of the enemy; send me troops." What more could you ask for if you had been defeated? "I have captured two of the enemy's camps, filled, of course, with plunder and supplies; send me corn and money." What more could you want if you had been despoiled, stripped of your own camp? And that I may not be the only one to be surprised at your delight—for as I have answered Himilco [a pro-Barcid Carthaginian counselor], I have a perfect right to ask questions in my turn—I should be glad if either Himilco or Mago would tell me, since, you say, the Battle of Cannae has all but destroyed the power of Rome and the whole of Italy is admittedly in revolt, whether, in the first place, any single community of the Latin nation has come over to us, and, secondly, whether a single man out of the thirty-five Roman tribes has deserted to Hannibal.' Mago answered both questions in the negative. 'Then there are still,' Hanno continued, 'far too many of the enemy left. But I should like to know how much courage and confidence that vast multitude possess.' Hanno followed up this stinging inquisition by asking if the Romans were now suing for peace. Clearly savoring Mago's negative response, Hanno retorted that it was clear that the war was far from won. Despite the obvious power of his words, however, the Council voted to send

Hannibal a force of 4,000 Numidians and 40 elephants, as well as 500 talents of silver. The situation on the island of Sicily was now beginning to look favorable. At Syracuse, the death of Rome's loyal ally Hiero and the subsequent ascension in 215 BC of his teenage grandson Hieronymus to the throne had presented an opportunity for the Carthaginians.

Under the influence of pro-Carthaginian advisers, the young king had made friendly overtures to Hannibal, and the latter promptly sent two of his officers of Syracusan origin, the brothers Hippocrates and Epicydes, to Sicily to negotiate an alliance. While Hieronymus was soon dramatically assassinated, and a pro-Carthaginian coup in Syracuse was suppressed, Hippocrates and Epicydes were nevertheless elected to the city's council. As the cities of Sicily wavered between support for Rome and support for Carthage, the brothers used their position to foment anti-Roman feeling among the Syracusan army and citizenry (as well as elsewhere on the island), and were eventually elected as the city's generals. A Roman army immediately invaded Syracusan territory and set up camp at the city's walls. The Roman general Marcellus then demanded that the Syracusans immediately hand over the brothers, accept back the pro-Roman politicians who had fled, and restore the previous pro-Roman government. With his ultimatum rejected, Marcellus had little option but to attempt to capture the city, and when an initial assault in the winter of 213 failed, a siege that was to last for more than a year began.

The situation would further improve for the Carthaginians when a considerable number of other Sicilian cities also rebelled against Rome in 213, no doubt encouraged by the arrival of a 30,000-strong Punic army on the island. On Sardinia, by contrast, a rebellion in support of Hannibal was swiftly suppressed. In Spain, the Scipio brothers were enjoying some success against the well-established Carthaginian forces. First they had managed to prevent Hasdrubal from leaving the peninsula to lend support to his brother Hannibal in Italy by inflicting a heavy defeat on his forces at Hibera in 216. And, despite the arrival of reinforcements led by Mago (reinforcements originally earmarked for Italy), the sequence of Carthaginian defeats continued for the next three years. Thus by 212 the Scipios had tied up three Carthaginian armies in Spain. Despite the setbacks on Sardinia and in Spain, help had now come from an unexpected source. In the spring of 215 an embassy sent by Philip of Macedon had landed at Bruttium and traveled on to Campania to meet with Hannibal and agree to a treaty. Polybius claims to reproduce the actual treaty document, a copy of which reportedly fell into Roman hands when a ship carrying both Macedonian and Carthaginian officials was captured on its return to the East.

The terms of the treaty bound both sides to protect one another from each other's enemies, with the explicit understanding that the Macedonians would help the Carthaginians in their war against Rome until final victory had been won. Yet it is also clear from the terms that Hannibal was keen to limit Philip's intervention in the conflict and, overall, to keep the Macedonians out of Italy. Once victory was complete, the terms of Carthage's peace with Rome would apply to Macedonia also, with Philip gaining Rome's possessions in Illyria. The treaty text itself, which appears to have been translated from Punic into Greek by Hannibal's chancery, shows clear associations with the diplomatic language and conventions that had existed in the Near East for millennia, proving that the Levantine roots of the city still exerted a heavy influence on traditional aspects of state business. Appended to the treaty was a list of Carthaginian gods who acted as divine witnesses to the agreement, organized into three (presumably hierarchical) celestial triads. The identities of these deities, who have been transliterated into the Greek divine canon, have been much debated, but it is now generally thought that the top tier was composed of Baal

Hammon, Tanit and Reshef. In the second were Astarte, Melqart and Eshmoun, followed by Baal Saphon, Hadad and Baal Malagê in the third. What is particularly interesting about this celestial ordering is that it reflects the divine patrons of the city of Carthage, and not of the Barcids.

When it came to negotiating with Philip, king of one of the most powerful of the Hellenistic kingdoms, even Hannibal's reputation as a great general was not enough. This had to be an alliance between Macedonia and Carthage, hence the presence of three named Carthaginian officials—Mago, Myrcan and Barmocar, who were either members of the Tribunal of One Hundred and Four or part of a special commission appointed by that body—as well as other, unnamed, counselors This treaty was just one of a number of signs that deference to the constitutional bodies of Carthage had come increasingly to replace the autonomy of action that had marked much of Hannibal's early career. The huge level of financial support that Hannibal received from North Africa in this period demanded the constant involvement of the Carthaginian Council. It is striking that it was not until the last years of his time in Italy that Hannibal seems to have produced any coinage himself, meaning that he was relying on booty, promises of pay after victory, and coinage being shipped in from Carthage. All of Carthage's resources were thus thrown at the war effort.

Chapter 12: To the Gates of Rome

At Rome the war campaign was causing significant economic strain. Following a set of devaluations in 217 along with the subsequent urgent manufacture of an issue of gold currency, the coinage system was thoroughly reorganized. Nevertheless even this strict proceeding did not defend the new silver denarius, the focal point of the new currency, from two succeeding devaluations. Even a doubling of the income tax rates, large financial loans from Hiero of Syracuse and the establishing of a state financial institution had not been sufficient to meet the increasing expense of the campaign, and by 215 loans with an extra risk premium had to be set up with private tax-gathering syndicates. On top of that, edicts were passed in 214 and 210 which in turn put in place enforced progressive taxation of Rome's wealthiest citizens specifically to pay for the fitting out of Rome's navy. The catastrophic defeats of 217/216 forced a reform of the armed forces. The terrible losses in the legions were balanced out by the recruitment of those who had previously been ineligible for military service. Therefore the new legions included slaves and criminals, and there might also have been a lowering of the requisite property criteria in order to incorporate the Roman poor. Indeed, at its height, it is thought that the Roman army during this time period may have numbered as many as 100,000 infantry, 7,500 cavalry along with an equal amount of allied troops. Most importantly of all, there appears to have also been a mindful effort to sustain more continuity in the senior command. Thus Fabius Maximus, who had previously caused Hannibal so many problems, would unusually hold a third, fourth and then a fifth consulship in 215, 214 and 209, while another three veteran commanders held the same office another two or three times between 215 and 209. Despite such reforms, the city nonetheless remained in the grip of a panic caused by the proximity of the Carthaginian army in southern Italy, a panic compounded by the appearance of a number of menacing religious portents. In 216 the decision had therefore been made to send the senator (and future historian) Quintus Fabius Pictor to the famous sanctuary of Delphi, to discover what prayers and supplications might appease the anger of the gods. The instructions with which Fabius Pictor returned from the oracle specified offerings to particular deities and stipulated that upon final victory the Romans should dedicate a portion of the war booty to Delphic Apollo.

The decision to consult the oracle was a clever move on the part of the Senate: not only did it publicly affirm Rome's cultural links with the Greek world (in the face of a Carthaginian attempt to undermine such links), it also made that affirmation at a time when Hannibal was menacing the cities of Magna Graecia. It therefore sought to re-establish firmly Rome's Greek credentials. At the same time, however, the Romans now performed a religious rite which was unmistakably their own. Turning to their Books of Fate, they revived the terrible ritual whereby a Gallic man and woman and a Greek man and woman were buried alive in the Forum Boarium, in what Livy disapprovingly described as 'a sacrifice wholly alien to the Roman spirit'. Roman human sacrifice was, however, not a crass anachronism, but something first recorded just a few years previously, in 228, when the city was faced by Gallic invasion. Its instigation now was surely a measure of the panic that Hannibal's success had engendered in the city.

Hannibal spent much of 213 in the pleasant surroundings of Apulia and Campania, without making the impact for which he may have hoped. Furthermore, worrying news that the Romans were besieging Syracuse soon arrived. The city was ably defended by the extraordinary range of weapons developed by its chief engineer, Archimedes, the ancient's world's most brilliant geometrician, but by the spring of

212 the Roman commander, Marcellus, had not only managed to bring many rebellious cities to heel, but had also breached Syracuse's outer fortification wall.

Later in the summer the Romans also managed to beat off a substantial Punic Sicilian army, which was then further decimated by plague, killing the general Hippocrates. A further Carthaginian force sent to the island in an attempt to retrieve this deteriorating situation failed dismally, and even Epicydes, sensing the increasing hopelessness of the position, slipped away. After botched peace negotiations, Syracuse eventually fell to the Romans through the treachery of some mercenary leaders. Although the property of pro-Roman citizens was protected, the city was extensively looted and many were killed, including the great Archimedes (despite Marcellus' specific instructions that he should be spared).

The fall of Syracuse meant that Carthaginian hopes in Sicily were all but snuffed out, and the failure of the Sicilian revolt was a bitter blow. Not least, Carthage had invested heavily in it, even striking two very large issues of coinage specifically to be used during the campaign. For Hannibal, the loss of Syracuse and the decline of Carthaginian fortunes in Sicily was only one of a number of pressing problems, of which the most worrying was the Roman seizure of a number of towns in Apulia. And yet now, as so often before, just when the Italian campaign had begun to flounder, fortune decided to smile kindly on the Carthaginian general, for Tarentum, the most important city in Magna Graecia, dramatically capitulated. Both main historical sources for the Second Punic War carry such detailed descriptions of the events surrounding the capture of the city that it is generally accepted that such descriptions derived from the pen of Silenus. Tarentum had long been a target for Hannibal, but, although there were pro-Carthaginian sympathizers within its walls, they had never been strong enough to deliver the city.

By 212, however, feelings were running high against Rome owing to an incident in which a number of Tarentine hostages had been executed by the Romans after trying to escape. Hannibal was at the time camped close to the city, when one evening a group of Tarentine young men left the town and approached the Carthaginian lines. Their leaders, Philemenus and Nicon, were brought before Hannibal and explained that they wished to surrender the city to him. After encouraging them and arranging a secret location for further meetings, Hannibal gave the Tarentine conspirators some cattle so that it would look as if they had successfully stolen them from his camp, thereby alleviating any suspicions on the part of the Roman guard.

During a second rendezvous, an agreement was reached with the plotters that on the capture of the city the Carthaginians would respect all Tarentine rights and property. Now an elaborate plan to capture the city by stealth was set in motion. Over a number of nights

Philemenus, who was a renowned hunter, left the city purportedly looking for game. By giving some of his catch to the Roman sentries, he gained their trust enough that they would open the gate at the sound of his whistle. An evening when the commander of the Roman garrison was hosting a party was chosen for the seizure of the city. First, an elite Carthaginian force of 10,000 men left their camp and covered three days' march in one session. Hannibal then carefully disguised this troop movement by sending a squadron of Numidian cavalry ahead so that it appeared that this was nothing more than a raid. Meanwhile, some of the Tarentine conspirators had attended the Roman commander's party and ensured that the celebrations had gone on late into the night. Other plotters gathered around the main gate of Tarentum, and when a fire signal was given from outside by Hannibal they rushed the guards stationed there and killed them before admitting the waiting Carthaginians.

At the second gate, which Philemenus had used for his nocturnal forays, Hannibal's troops burst in and killed the sentries while they were admiring Philemenus' catch, a huge boar being carried on a stretcher. After ordering that all the citizens should be spared, Hannibal sent his troops to secure the city. Then at daybreak he summoned all the Tarentines to the marketplace and gave them assurances that they would not be harmed. While the spectacular capture of Tarentum led to an immediate revival in Carthaginian fortunes, it was however salted by two major difficulties. First, much of the city's Roman garrison, including its commander, had managed to take refuge in the citadel, which stood in an almost unassailable position with access to the sea. There they would remain while Tarentum was in Carthaginian hands.

Second, and far more seriously, Capua was now under siege by four Roman legions with orders from the Senate to remain there until the city was taken. In spring 211, after he had failed to break through the Roman encirclement, Hannibal's hand was finally forced. Only one course of action could now draw Roman troops away from Capua. He would march on Rome. In order to ensure that the Latin cities understood that Rome could not now protect them, Hannibal left a trail of devastation as he marched north.

In Rome, panic reigned as news of the Carthaginian advance reached the city, and Hannibal deliberately raised the level of hysteria by sending his Numidian horsemen to terrorize the refugees trying to flee there. Matters only got worse when a squadron of Numidian deserters who had been ordered by the Romans to mobilize against Hannibal's force were mistaken for the enemy by the terrified citizens. Livy reported that 'The wailing cry of the matrons was heard everywhere, not only in private houses but even in the temples. Here they knelt and swept the temple floors with their disheveled hair and lifted up their hands to heaven in piteous entreaty to the gods that they would deliver the city of Rome out of the hands of the enemy and preserve its mothers and children from injury and outrage.' As a further indication of the seriousness of the situation, the Senate went into emergency sitting and troops were posted around the city.

The panic reached its climax when Hannibal himself—seven years after first entering Italy—finally approached the walls of Rome at the Colline Gate, accompanied by 2,000 Numidian horsemen. If we believe the accounts of Polybius and Livy, however, what transpired next was something of an anticlimax. The former claims (unconvincingly) that the victor of Cannae was dissuaded from attacking the city by the appearance of a legion of battle-ready new recruits. In Livy's account of the episode, however, Hannibal was discouraged by the onset of a severe hailstorm on consecutive days, which he took to be an unfavorable divine omen. He was supposedly further demoralized by the news that the Romans took his challenge so lightly that they were diverting troops to fight in Spain, and that the very land on which his army was camped had been recently sold at auction, with no shortage of Roman buyers, such was the confidence in victory.

According to Livy, Hannibal responded by ordering a herald to auction off all the financiers' pitches around the Roman forum. Both these accounts are based, however, on little more than willful misunderstandings of Hannibal's true motives. In terms of military strategy the march upon Rome had been a success, because 15,000 Roman troops, under the command of Quintus Fulvius Flaccus, had been summoned back from Capua to defend the city, even if neither Hannibal nor the Roman commanders expected an assault on it (Hannibal had, after all, left most of his heavy infantry and equipment behind at his base in Bruttium). More importantly, Hannibal's presence at the walls of Rome served a crucial propagandist function. One of the few references to have survived from the history of

Silenus, Hannibal's loyal chronicler, gives an extraordinary insight into the significance of the Carthaginian's visit to the gates of Rome. In this fragment Silenus gives an account of Hercules' sojourn in Rome which is markedly at variance with other tales of the hero's visit. In the Silenian version, Rome's famous Palatine Hill was named after Palantho, daughter of Hyperboreos, the eponymous leader of the Hyperboreans, a mythical northern people. She had enjoyed a romantic liaison with Hercules on that very spot, and hence the hill had gained its name. In another tale, also thought to have derived from Silenus, Latinus, first king and founder of the Latin people, was the product of that same union between Palantho and Hercules. In the charged atmosphere of the Hannibalic war, this seemingly obscure point of history had very serious propaganda implications.

Silenus' version of the prehistory of Rome directly contradicted the generally accepted Roman version of events, which told that

Latinus' mother was Fauna, the wife of Faunus, the indigenous king of the region. In Silenus' account, furthermore, the Hyperboreans appear as a metaphor for the Gauls, the barbarous people whom Hercules himself had supposedly tamed on his journey across the Alps. Now Hannibal had crossed that great mountain chain with an army full of Gauls. It therefore looked as if 'history' would repeat itself, as Hercules and his Hyperboreans returned to the Palatine to claim what was rightfully theirs. Part of that Herculean patrimony included the Latins, the product of the ancient union between the hero and his Hyperborean lover. Silenus' re-conception of Roman prehistory and the display of power which the destructive march to Rome represented were therefore part of the same determined campaign to detach the Latins from Rome. It was no coincidence that, as he approached the walls of Rome, Hannibal had first stopped at the temple of Hercules by the Colline Gate. He wanted those who looked on to know that a new Hercules had also journeyed there, with a divine mandate to free the region's people from the heirs of Cacus who had terrorized them for so long. The decision taken by Fabius Maximus in 209/208 to have the temple of Hercules moved to the safety of the Capitol strongly suggests that Hannibal's visit had been something of a propaganda coup.

For all its ideological impact, however, the march on Rome had not achieved its major strategic aim, for at Capua in 211 the demoralized Senate had nonetheless surrendered to the Roman army, and paid a heavy price for its treachery. Anxious to make an example of the city, the Romans rounded up the leaders of the pro-Carthaginian faction and then scourged and executed them. All the other citizens were sold into slavery. The city itself was not completely destroyed, but was allowed to carry on as a humble agricultural market town under the direct rule of Roman officials, a mere shadow of its former self. Indeed, the name of Capua was thereafter associated in the Roman imagination with the conceit of pride and the dangers of ambition. The impact of the loss of Capua was felt across the region, with a number of other Carthaginian-held towns falling to the Romans. Hannibal continued to enjoy some military success, however, most notably the defeat of a Roman army at Herdonea in 210, which resulted in the death of its general the proconsul Gnaeus Fulvius Centumalus, many of his senior officers and thousands of troops.

But by 209 even Tarentum had been lost, and the enormous amount of war booty captured from the city helped rescue Rome from the financial crisis in which it had been embroiled. The Romans now fought back in other ways. Fabius Maximus, the victorious Roman general, placed a colossal statue of Hercules captured at Tarentum on the Capitol, near to a bronze equestrian statue of himself. The relocation of the statue not only played to Fabius' much trumpeted family connections to the hero, but also reclaimed Hercules for the Roman cause. It was another member of the Fabii clan, Fabius Pictor, the senator who had been sent to Delphi in 216, who completed the first history of Rome by a Roman historian–his celebrated Annales (which has unfortunately not survived).

Following the literary conventions of the day, Pictor wrote his opus in Greek. It is clear that he had read the western-Greek historians, such as Timaeus and Philinus, and had accepted the theory that the Romans were the descendants of the Trojans. Yet at the same time Pictor construed his work as a radical departure from the Greek-authored works that had preceded it. This was unashamedly a Roman history. As well as highlighting his use of Roman documentary sources for his research, Pictor also provided careful explanations of archaic Roman customs. The strong emphasis on traditional Roman culture was further underlined by the presentation of the work in the form of annals, a kind of official record traditionally used by the Romans to set down election results, religious ceremonies and other official notices. Despite the Romano-centric hue of his work, however, Pictor, who was a committed philhellene, wrote with a Greek as well as an educated Roman audience in mind. Indeed, one of the major aims of his project was to remind the inhabitants of mainland Greece and Magna Graecia that Rome had a distinguished past which represented far more than a pale reflection of the Hellenic world. The statement of Rome's cultural equality to Greece was, however, only one part of Fabius Pictor's agenda.

He wrote his history during some of the most difficult moments of the war against Hannibal, probably finishing it around 210. The first Roman history was thus written at a time when the Romans were bearing the brunt of a morale-sapping assault not only on the battlefield, but also on their collective identity. Their relationships with their gods, their allies and the wider Mediterranean world had all been called into question by potent Carthaginian propaganda. Indeed, it is probably the Hannibalic context which explains Polybius' complaint that Pictor showed too much of a pro-Roman bias in his work. In this time of crisis, Pictor attempted to show both Rome and its allies just how spectacularly successful the Romans had been. After relating the arrival of Aeneas and the Trojans in Italy, Pictor's Annales described their first foundation at Alba Longa, the eventual establishment of Rome just to the north of this, and other traditional stories such as the rape of the Sabine women. Those stories stressed not only Rome's antiquity but also its historic and deep-seated ties with the other cities of Latium, key allies in the fight against Hannibal. Furthermore, the cultural links between southern Greeks and Romans were consolidated by reference to Evander, the leader of the Arcadian Greeks who had first settled the site of Rome. Most significantly of all, Pictor is accredited with having given a detailed description of the activities of Hercules, presumably in Italy and specifically at the site of

Rome. Within the context of Hannibal's own particular claims to the Herculean mantle, that description represented an attempt to re-situate the legend firmly within Roman foundational history.

Chapter 13: The Legacy of Scipio

In Spain there had been some hope of a revival in Carthaginian fortunes with the defeat and deaths of both Publius and Gnaeus Scipio in 211. The leaderless Roman forces, however, had rallied strongly under Lucius Marcius Septimus, irregularly proclaimed as leader by the troops. Furthermore, the capture of Capua had meant that many of the troops that had been involved in its siege could now be reassigned to Spain, and a new commander to oversee Roman forces in Spain was subsequently elected. The selection was controversial for a number of reasons. The consuls, unusually, brought their nomination before the Popular Assembly for validation, and their candidate should have been disbarred because he had not previously held the requisite senior senatorial post. Indeed, it appears that the powerful Cornelii clan had arranged things so that no one else would stand against Publius Cornelius Scipio, the 25-year-old son and nephew of the two dead generals. Although this may appear little more than nepotism, Scipio's appointment was a shrewd move, for there was no doubt that the Roman armies in Spain would welcome a Scipio as their new commander. It was also apparent, even at this early stage of his career, that the young Scipio was an exceptional man.

Scipio was a member of a younger generation of junior Roman senators who had gained their experience solely against an enemy whose sophisticated use of military and propagandist strategies was a clear advance on previous opposition. Much of Scipio's genius came from his capacity to borrow and even improve upon many of the strategies that Hannibal himself had deployed to such great effect. This included not only military but also ideological tactics, for Scipio appears to have believed that the most effective way to counter the widely held belief in Hannibal's divine sanction was to encourage the idea that he himself enjoyed heroic status and divine favor. Stories thus went into circulation which connected Scipio's conception and subsequent life with the gods: Scipio was believed to be the son of Jupiter; for before he was conceived a serpent appeared in his mother's bed, and a snake crawled over him when he was an infant without doing him any harm. When he went back late to the Capitol, the dogs never barked at him.

He never started out on any course of action without first having sat for a long time in the shrine of Jupiter, as if to receive the god's instruction. It is, of course, not difficult to see that these stories, which appear in a number of different ancient authors, were designed to create an association both with Alexander the Great and, primarily, with Hercules (himself the son of Zeus/Jupiter). This constituted a direct challenge to a Hannibalic campaign that cast the Carthaginian general in the same light. Another story reported that when his elder brother Lucius stood for the aedileship, Scipio managed to secure election both for his sibling and himself by telling his mother that he had twice dreamed that this would come about, prompting Polybius to comment that 'people now believed that he communed with the gods not only in reality and by day, but still more in his sleep.' Scipio's rumored quasi-divinity demonstrates the extent to which the Roman people linked political and military success with divine favor (as in the case of Hannibal). While skeptical historians in the mold of Livy or Polybius might dismiss such associations as nothing more than gossip or superstition, it nonetheless seems clear that Scipio himself actively encouraged them. Certainly Livy, despite condemning the tales about Scipio's miraculous birth as nothing more than gossip, strongly suggests that the Roman general did not discourage the impression that he enjoyed divine favor: He himself never made light of men's belief in these marvels; on the contrary it was rather promoted by a certain studied practice of neither denying such a thing nor openly asserting it. Many other things of the same sort, some true, some pretended, had passed the limits of admiration for a mere man in the case of this youth. Such were things upon which the citizens relied when they entrusted to any age far from mature the great responsibility of so great a command. Scipio's strategic manipulation of his heroic reputation is aptly demonstrated by events at the siege of New Carthage in 209.

After learning that none of the Carthaginian armies operating on the Iberian peninsula was within ten days' march of the city, Scipio decided to attack. It was a bold but clever move, because if he were successful it would rob the Carthaginian commanders of a strategically important base and, furthermore, seriously weaken the Barcid reputation in Spain. Stationing his fleet opposite New Carthage, Scipio encouraged its defenders to think that an attack was to be mounted from the eastern, landward, side of the city by throwing up command more sanguine and more ready to face dangerous enterprises by instilling in them the belief that his projects were divinely inspired'. In Scipio, Hannibal thus found an opponent who not only provided a stiff challenge on the battlefield, but also presented himself as a serious rival for the Carthaginian's divine/heroic mantle.

In another indication that he had learned much from Hannibal, Scipio showed mercy to the inhabitants of New Carthage and let many of them return home. He also solved his own manpower problems by promising eventual liberty to the Carthaginian soldiers if they served on his warships and on labor details. The Spanish hostages whom he found in New Carthage were assured of their freedom to return home if their peoples became Roman allies. And the Roman cause in Spain was further boosted by the enormous amount of captured booty: over 600 talents of silver and a vast quantity of war munitions, as well as a fully operational mint

earthworks there. In fact the attack would con
from the west, for he had learned from local
fishermen that the lagoon which bordered tha
side of the city was fairly shallow, and further
that during the ebb of the tide, towards evenin
it emptied out through a narrow channel that
connected it to the sea. Scipio nevertheless tol(
his troops a very different story, for he related
how Neptune, the Roman sea god, had appeare
to him in a dream and promised his assistance
capturing the city. The next day, after first
launching a fierce assault on the city from the
east in order to divert the attention of the
Carthaginian defenders, Scipio ordered 500 of
his men to cross the lagoon with ladders. After
wading through the now shallow waters, the me
quickly scaled the unguarded western walls.
With Roman troops inside the city itself, New
Carthage soon fell. The Neptune incident at the
siege of New Carthage conforms to a now
familiar model of myth-making as a strategic
weapon. Polybius saw this incident as an
example of how Scipio 'made the men under his

with which Scipio could immediately start issuing coinage. With these considerable resources at his disposal, Scipio now turned his attention to the three Carthaginian armies that were operating in Spain. A mass of defections to the Romans had led Hannibal's brother Hasdrubal to the conclusion that he had to attack Scipio as soon as possible. The two armies met in spring 208 at Baecula, in the north-west of the modern Spanish province of Jaén. Scipio, through bold and decisive action, soon got the better of Hasdrubal's forces, and the Carthaginian consequently put his reserve plan into operation, heading north with the remnants of his army with the intention of joining his brother in Italy. After this great and decisive victory, however, an embarrassing and potentially dangerous moment occurred when a number of Spanish chiefs acclaimed Scipio as king. This was a title that would not win much favor in Rome, where regal aspirations were hated and feared in equal measure. Scipio, however, responded with characteristic diplomacy: 'He ordered silence to be proclaimed, and then told them that the title he valued most was the one his soldiers had given him, the title of "Imperator". "The name of king," he said, "so great elsewhere, is insupportable to Roman ears. If a kingly mind is in your eyes the noblest thing in human nature, you may attribute it to me in thought, but you must avoid the use of the word."'

Despite Scipio's proclamation (mental or otherwise) as king, the Carthaginians were not yet spent, and had decided on a new course of action. While one army under Hasdrubal Gisco would attempt to hold the only part of the peninsula that remained loyal—the lower Guadalquivir valley and Gades—Mago would travel to the Balearic Islands to recruit fresh troops. Hasdrubal Barca, meanwhile, hurried north with the remainder of the Carthaginian forces, recruiting Gallic mercenaries as he went. After waiting until winter had passed, he and his Carthaginian army crossed the Alps into Italy, taking the easier route through the Durance and Mont Genèvre passes. With Hasdrubal departed for Italy, the Carthaginian position in Spain became increasingly desperate. A relief army sent from North Africa had been routed, leaving the remainder of the Carthaginian forces holed up in strongholds around Gades and the lower Guadalquivir valley.

In the spring of 206, Hannibal's brother Mago, now returned from the Balearics, had joined up with Hasdrubal Gisco and decided to stake all in open battle with Scipio at Ilipa. Although the Carthaginian army was numerically greater (with 60,000 troops compared with the Roman 50,000), Scipio proved himself to be every bit as daring and original a general as Hannibal. After first putting pressure on the Carthaginians by drawing his army up for battle at daybreak, Scipio, rather than placing his crack Roman legionaries in the center as was customary, stationed them on the flanks, with his less reliable Spanish auxiliaries at the center.

Using similar tactics to those of Hannibal at Cannae, therefore, Scipio let his battle line advance before ordering his legionaries on the wings to turn in on the center. When the Spanish federates on the enemy flanks had been driven back, pressure was then brought to bear on the Carthaginian center, which, after a hard fight, was eventually overthrown. After the final, desperate defeat at Ilipa, Carthaginian resistance in Spain quickly folded, with many of the senior command fleeing to their last real stronghold, Gades. Even the subsequent illness of Scipio, a troop mutiny and a revolt against Rome by the powerful Ilergetes tribes could not revive the Carthaginian cause. By the end of 206, Mago, who had already had to put down an insurrection in the previously loyal stronghold of Gades, left the Iberian peninsula to join Hannibal in Italy and the people of Gades surrendered to the Romans. The once glittering imperial possession that had been Barcid Spain was no more, after little more than thirty years of existence.

Chapter 14: One Must Fall

In 207 BC, even though the circumstances in Spain looked progressively favorable for the Romans, in Italy ominous prodigies had once again been widely witnessed: at Veii showers of rocks were reported; at Menturnae the temple of Jupiter ended up being struck by lightning; and at Capua a wolf had managed to sneak right into the city and mauled one of the sentries. Most dramatically, at Frusino a hermaphroditic child was born the same size as a four-year-old. Diviners summoned from Etruria proclaimed that the monstrous baby ought to be banished from Roman land without any contact with the earth. After being placed in a box, therefore, the ill-fated child was taken out to sea and thrown overboard. The priests of Rome also decreed that three bands of nine virgins should parade through the city chanting a hymn written for the event by the Tarentine poet Livius Andronicus. Andronicus was a shrewd choice for a couple of reasons. He previously authored the first-ever Roman play, which had been publicly commissioned and first performed in 240 in celebration of the victorious conclusion of the First Punic War, and he along with his work for that reason stood as a representation of Roman triumph over Carthage. As an effective Tarentine who wrote in Greek, furthermore, he exemplified Rome's strong links with the western-Greek world—links put under great strain, and in some cases totally severed, during the course of the war with Hannibal. For the Romans, again, re-establishing proper relations with the gods also demanded recapturing the propaganda initiative from the Carthaginians. Soon after events at Frusino, the temple of Juno Regina on Rome's Aventine Hill was struck by lightning. In response to her apparent anger, the goddess was propitiated with a solid-gold basin, paid for out of the dowries of the matrons of Rome, and celebrated with solemn sacrifices. Juno's implacable hostility to the Romans (and favor for the Carthaginians) became a very familiar theme in later Roman literature, but this was the first public acknowledgment of that supposed enmity.

Contemporary evidence suggests that Hannibal was at least partly responsible for the development of this tradition. While later Roman writers would identify Juno and Tanit, in this period an association had already been drawn in central Italy between Iuni, the Etruscan version of Juno, and the Punic goddess Astarte (on the Pyrgi Tablets). On at least two occasions, Hannibal performed sacred rites at Lake Avernus, a volcanic-crater lake in Campania, widely thought to be the gateway to the underworld and sacred to Avernus, god of death, the husband of the goddess Juno Averna. While it seems likely that Hannibal was worshiping Astarte at Avernus (or perhaps her divine consort Melqart), the Romans may have perceived his actions as an attempt to win over Juno to the Carthaginian cause. The religious rituals conducted at the temple of Juno Regina, therefore, once again point to the success of

Hannibal's assault upon the sacred landscape of Italy. The military situation was similarly portentous, for in the summer of 208 the two Roman consuls, Titus Quinctius Crispinus and Marcus Claudius Marcellus, had been killed. Marcellus' signet ring had, furthermore, fallen into the hands of Hannibal, who then tried to use it to recapture the city of Salapia by sending a letter proclaiming the imminent arrival of the (in fact dead) Roman general. Crispinus, Marcellus' consular colleague, had however managed before his death to warn the surrounding cities, so that when Hannibal arrived at Salapia he could not gain admittance, even with a contingent of Roman deserters placed deceptively in the vanguard. For the Romans it was crucial to prevent Hannibal and Hasdrubal from joining forces, and so Gaius Claudius Nero, one of the replacement consuls, was sent to contain the former in the south while his colleague Marcus Livius Salinator confronted the latter in the north. By early summer 207 Hasdrubal had successfully crossed the Alpine passes and reached the Po valley, with his army in good shape. For Rome this was a particularly dangerous moment, since the Latins, who had hitherto been loyal, had grown increasingly tired of the seemingly endless demands that were placed upon them, and in 208 twelve of the thirty Roman colonies in Latium had refused to provide subsidies and troops for the war effort. After wasting precious time on a failed siege of the Roman colony of Placentia, Hasdrubal collected more supplies and Gallic troops before marching down the Adriatic coast.

In Bruttium, Hannibal made preparations to go north to meet his brother. Although he managed to keep his army on the move, the Carthaginians suffered considerable losses when challenged by Roman forces on a number of occasions. Yet greater disaster awaited, however. A letter sent by Hasdrubal to Hannibal which outlined where the meeting between their respective armies should take place fell into Roman hands after the messengers mistakenly went to Roman-held Tarentum and were captured. After informing the Senate, the consul Claudius Nero secretly marched north with a considerable force, leaving the remaining Roman soldiers to obstruct Hannibal at the Apulian town of Canusium. After a series of forced marches, Nero reached the camp of his consular colleague Salinator at Sena Gallica in Umbria, close to where Hasdrubal was encamped. Despite Roman efforts to conceal the arrival of this new force, the Carthaginian general realized that something was wrong and hastily tried to retreat. However, his guides deserted, and the Romans were soon harrying the lost Carthaginian army as they searched for a place to cross the river Metaurus. The situation soon became so desperate that Hasdrubal was forced to make a stand. After brave resistance the Carthaginian lines were eventually broken, and Hasdrubal, knowing that all was lost, charged into the Roman lines and was killed.

Tragically, Hannibal learned of the defeat through the sight of his brother's severed head being hurled before his lines. With the prospect of victory fast disappearing, he mustered his army and retreated to his enclave in Bruttium. There he remained for the next few years living like a minor Hellenistic prince-ling, surrounded by the wreckage of his Italian dreams. Hannibal's misery was now compounded by the return of the victorious Scipio from Spain. Despite a masterful stage-managed account of his victories in front of the Senate at the temple of Bellona, and war booty totaling a massive 6,500 kilograms of silver, Scipio nevertheless failed to obtain a triumph, for he had never held a senior magistracy. Such was his popularity, however, that he easily won the election for the consulship in 205. Scipio now pushed hard to be granted North Africa as his field of operation, for he believed that the Carthaginians would be finished off only if defeated in their homeland. Others, led by Fabius Maximus, wanted to concentrate on first driving Hannibal out of

Italy, but eventually, after an increasingly heated debate, a compromise was reached. Scipio was allotted Sicily as his theater of command, but with the proviso that he could attack North Africa if it served the Senate's interests. His consular colleague, Publius Licinius Crassus, was to remain in Italy and keep the pressure on Hannibal. This arrangement clearly favored Scipio, and his senatorial opponents therefore tried to hamper his war preparations by refusing him the right to levy troops. Many, however, simply volunteered to fight under him, and a number of loyal Italian states provided timber for ships, as well as corn and munitions. Scipio was thus able to proceed to Sicily to train his army for the battle in North Africa. Defeated in Spain, Hannibal's brother Mago landed at Liguria in the spring of 205, bringing with him 12,000 infantry and 2,000 cavalry. By that summer, after receiving further reinforcements from Carthage and from among the Gauls and Ligurians, he was ready to move south.

The Romans, however, now experienced in dealing with such a threat, simply blocked both sides of the Apennines, meaning that for the next two years Mago and his army were effectively trapped in northern Italy. Hannibal also could do little but wait in his enclave at Bruttium, for he found himself increasingly blockaded both by sea and by land. In the summer of 205 eighty Carthaginian transport ships bound for Bruttium were captured, and no help could be expected from his 'ally' Philip of Macedon: through a series of treaties with Philip's enemies in Greece and Asia Minor the Romans had cleverly ensured that Philip was far too preoccupied at home to contemplate an intervention, and in 205, with the pressure mounting, he had hastily sued for peace with Rome and its allies, thereby jettisoning his previous treaty with Carthage. The Roman Senate now sensed that the fragile alliance of Carthaginians, Italians and Greeks which Hannibal had constructed was poised to dissolve. It therefore undertook two ideologically charged missions which brilliantly emphasized the cultural links between Rome, Italy and Greece. The Senate now decided to fulfill the promise of a share in the booty for the oracle at Delphi made over ten years previously. Two ambassadors were sent over to Greece with a golden wreath weighing 90 kilograms and other silver trophies from the spoils of the victory over Hasdrubal. Around the same time, a high-ranking Roman delegation was making its way eastward to receive a religious relic from Attalus, king of Pergamum. The object which they were to bring back to their city was a sacred stone of the earth goddess, Cybele (whom the Romans called Magna Mater, 'the Great Mother'). Earlier in 205, continued religious portents had led to another consultation of the sacred Sibylline books. Found within their hallowed pages was a prophecy that foretold the final defeat of Hannibal if the Magna Mater was returned to Rome. Some have puzzled at the timing of this prophecy, particularly as Hannibal was by now a spent force.

But great unease still lingered at Rome long after final victory on the battlefield seemed assured. Indeed, Hannibal's most lasting impact on Rome was not the bloody defeats that he inflicted on its legions at the Trebia, Lake Trasimene or Cannae, but his successful appropriation of much of the mythological legacy (particularly the Herculean legacy) that had acted as the keystone both in Rome's cultural and political affiliation with the Greek world and in its subsequent claims to the leadership of the central and western Mediterranean. The missions both to Delphi and, in particular, to bring back the Magna Mater therefore marked the beginnings of a protracted exorcism of the doubts and insecurities that Hannibal and his advisers had so skillfully planted in the collective consciousness of the Roman elite. The original home of the Magna Mater had been Mount Ida near Troy, and later myth would claim that Aeneas and his followers had once taken refuge there at the beginning of the journey to Rome. The journey to Pergamum and the negotiations for the sacred stone were thus a very public reaffirmation of Rome's heritage within the wider Hellenistic world, and by extension a reiteration of the historical and cultural connections that Hannibal had worked so hard to dismantle. By 204, after having his proconsular command extended for another year, Scipio was ready to take the war to North Africa. He had spent his time on Sicily carefully preparing for the invasion. As well as undertaking the important task of training and drilling his expeditionary force, he had also found the time to cross back to Italy in 205 and had recaptured the Calabrian town of Locri, thus keeping up the pressure on Hannibal. He had also traveled to North Africa, in order to visit Syphax, the king of the powerful Massaesylian Numidian kingdom, at his capital of Siga. Mindful that they would need friends in North Africa if the invasion was to be a success, the Romans had been assiduously courting this wily political operator since as early as 213. However, Syphax, although continuing to maintain friendly relations with Rome, had clearly calculated that for the time being it was safer to stay in an alliance with Carthage, which was still better placed to have a direct impact on his realm. Now, as the time for the great Roman invasion approached, Scipio made another attempt to detach the king from the Carthaginians.

By an extraordinary coincidence, his old Punic opponent from Spain, Hasdrubal Gisco, was also at Siga, having arrived there on his way back to Carthage. Syphax, juggling the competing claims of these two great powers as skillfully as ever, managed to persuade both the Roman general and his Carthaginian adversary to enjoy his hospitality together. Hasdrubal was reportedly so impressed by his Roman counterpart that he left for Carthage in fear for the future of his homeland. Scipio had nonetheless made the same miscalculation as his predecessors (including his late father and uncle) when he departed from Siga thinking that he had secured Syphax's support in the upcoming North African campaign. Hasdrubal Gisco, aware of the temptation the Roman overture would present to the Numidian king, had re-cemented the bonds between Carthage and Syphax by offering his daughter Sophonisba in marriage. Desire would succeed where diplomacy had failed, for the old king fell passionately in love with his lively, intelligent and beautiful young queen. A new alliance between the Massaesylians and Carthage was subsequently signed, after which Hasdrubal persuaded the king to send a message to Scipio in Sicily informing him of the new pact. Even after this disappointment, the odds were still very much stacked in Scipio's favor. While the Carthaginians had no real standing army in North Africa, and Hannibal's force was languishing in Bruttium, the invasion force of 35,000 men that Scipio had mobilized was a formidable proposition. At its heart were two legions of battle-hardened veterans who had spent the previous decade in exile, fighting in Sicily as a punishment for fleeing the field at

Cannae. This group, we are told, were particularly eager to make amends for their previous transgression. In the spring of 204 the expeditionary force left Lilybaeum to make the crossing to North Africa in a flotilla of 400 transport carriers with a guard of 20 warships. However, unfavorable weather forced Scipio to land the force near the city of Utica, to the north of Carthage, rather than at Syrtis Minor to the south, which would have exposed the fertile region of Cap Bon. The Carthaginians, although they must have predicted an imminent invasion, were still unprepared and, in an attempt to stall the Roman army while they mustered their own forces and awaited Syphax's Numidian contingents, they sent out two separate cavalry detachments to engage the enemy. Both forces were easily defeated. The Carthaginians were nevertheless saved by the close of the campaigning season, and Scipio, after failing to take the well-fortified Utica and conscious that the Carthaginian army was now finally assembled, withdrew and set up camp for the winter.

Realizing that the Carthaginian army would be a much weaker proposition without its Numidian cavalry, Scipio used the lull in fighting to make another attempt at luring Syphax over to the Roman side. The king, clearly concerned about the instability that a war in North Africa could bring to his own realm, was by this time far more anxious to broker a truce between Carthage and Rome (based on mutual withdrawal from the other's homeland). But Scipio, anxious for more personal glory and sensing that a definitive victory could be won, merely feigned interest in this proposition while secretly having an officer reconnoiter the enemy camps. From the information gleaned from this scouting operation, he resolved to launch a surprise attack on the Carthaginian and Numidian positions. One night, after setting up a diversion, Scipio attacked the camps by setting fire to the huts—made out of extremely flammable wood and foliage or reeds—where the Carthaginian and Numidian troops lived, with the result that much of the enemy army of 50,000 infantry and 13,000 cavalry was killed. This disastrous blow to the Carthaginian cause was followed several months later, in 203, by another major defeat at the hands of Scipio, this time in open battle on the great plains south of Utica. The Carthaginian Council of Elders now had little option but to play their final card, and summoned Hannibal back from Italy.

The Carthaginians stalled for time while they awaited Hannibal's arrival. They sent a thirty-man commission to Scipio at Tunes with a mandate to discuss treaty terms. After first prostrating themselves in front him in the Levantine tradition, the envoys proceeded to accept full responsibility for their present predicament, before then laying much of the blame for Carthage's actions on the Barcid clan and their supporters. In response, Scipio offered the following terms: the Carthaginians were to hand over all their prisoners of war as well as any deserters and refugees; they were to withdraw their armies from Italy, Gaul and Spain, and evacuate all the islands between Italy and Africa; they were to surrender their entire navy with the exception of twenty vessels, and provide huge quantities of wheat and barley to the Roman army; and finally they were to pay an indemnity of 5,000 talents of silver. These strictures were undoubtedly harsh, but previously Scipio had been determined to reject any peace proposals and destroy the city of Carthage itself. He had probably changed his mind only after his failure to take Utica, when he had realized that any siege of Carthage would be time-consuming and expensive in terms of both lives and material resources. And a long-drawn-out siege also presented the danger that Scipio himself might be replaced by another magistrate before final victory. The Carthaginian Council of Elders accepted the terms, and in the late summer of 203 a delegation was sent to Rome to conclude the treaty with the Senate. The ambassadors, apparently following an agreed strategy, once more blamed the Barcids for their present woes: 'He [Hannibal] had no orders from their Senate to cross the Hiberus, much less the Alps. It was on his own authority that he had made war not only on Rome but even on Saguntum; anyone who took a just view would recognize that the treaty with Rome remained unbroken to that day.' After absolving the Carthaginian Council of Elders of any responsibility for the war, the envoys argued that it was not Carthage but in fact Hannibal who had first broken the terms of 241.

The purpose of this rhetoric became clear when they proceeded to request that it should be only that treaty that was recognized–a far more advantageous arrangement, because it would have left the Carthaginians free to continue in the Balearic Islands and perhaps even southern Spain. Having ensured that the Roman offensive would be suspended while negotiations were ongoing, therefore, the envoys were now attempting to secure a better deal. Even if that deal was rejected, the longer their discussions continued, the more time Hannibal and Mago would have to return to North Africa. The Roman senators were no fools, however, and poured scorn on the transparent Carthaginian tactics (not least because it soon became clear that the Carthaginian delegation were too young to remember the actual terms of the 241 treaty). But, incredibly, motivated perhaps by suspicion both of Hannibal and of the ever-successful Scipio, the Senate grudgingly ratified the new treaty, with the proviso that it should come into force only when the armies of Mago and Hannibal had finally left Italy. Hannibal reacted to the command to evacuate bitterly. The blame game had long since begun in the Council of Elders, but Hannibal quickly showed that he too was not averse to finding an appropriate scapegoat. According to Livy: It is said that he gnashed his teeth, groaned, and almost shed tears when he heard what the delegates had to say. After they had delivered their instructions, he exclaimed, 'The men who tried to drag me back by cutting off my supplies of men and money are now recalling me not by crooked means but plainly and openly. So you see, it is not the Roman people who have been so often routed and cut to pieces that have vanquished Hannibal, but the Carthaginian Senate by their detraction and envy. It is not Scipio who will pride himself and exult over the disgrace of my return so much as Hanno who has crushed my house, since he could do it in no other way, beneath the ruins of Carthage.' Mutual recriminations continued to fly between the Barcids and their opponents as the fragile accord built on Hannibal's previous success began to fracture. Yet the Council of Elders had never been simply split between pro- and anti-Barcid factions, for many of the latter had been willing to support Hannibal while his aggressive strategy had brought prestige, booty and conquered territory. Once the bad news had started to arrive from the various Carthaginian fronts, the euphoria had quickly been replaced by growing concern and then anger. By 203, many who had previously been content to bask in the glory of Hannibal's achievements had now joined the ever-louder chorus of disapproval emanating from Hanno and his supporters. Hannibal nevertheless obeyed the command to return. His brother Mago, however, never reached his homeland, for, though he successfully embarked his troops in Liguria, he himself died of battle wounds as the fleet passed Sardinia, and a significant number of his ships were captured by the Romans. Hannibal landed in North Africa with an army composed of 15,000–20,000 experienced veterans. He had left some troops behind to garrison the few towns and cities that still remained loyal to him, and had released others entirely from his service. The Romans now moved to undermine the memory of Hannibal's considerable support in Italy, as well as the divine favoritism which his cause had claimed. A story was circulated which told how he had massacred his Italian troops when, refusing to embark for Africa, they had sought refuge in the temple of Juno at Cape Lacinium. Although the story was surely apocryphal, it is likely that its setting was carefully chosen by those who sought to blacken Hannibal's name, for it had been at that temple, just 10 kilometers away from his last base at Croton, that the Carthaginian general had sought to secure his Italian legacy by erecting a bronze tablet listing his achievements on the peninsula, in both Latin and Greek. Polybius, a visitor to the temple, proclaimed his trust in the accuracy of the troop and animal numbers that it presented.

However, he also intimated that other information it contained, which he did not include, was of a more dubious nature. This is not the only clue that Hannibal and his advisers, as they whiled away the days in their last stronghold at Bruttium, had come to see this famous sanctuary of Juno as a useful prop in their attempts to secure the lasting legacy of their campaign in Italy. The site was well known for the supernatural happenings that took place:

there was, for example, an altar in the entrance court where the ashes were never stirred by the wind. Yet it was also an extremely pleasant spot, with an enclosure surrounded by dense woodland, and its center blessed with rich pasture on which a variety of different breeds of cattle, sacred to the goddess, grazed. Such was the security and seclusion of the place that the cattle had no need of a cowherd, but simply took themselves back to their stalls at the end of the day. A portion of the huge profits made from the sale of these beasts had been used to pay for the making of a column of solid gold which was then dedicated to Juno. A story, attributed to the Roman historian Coelius, but thought by most scholars to have originated from Silenus, told of how Hannibal had wanted to carry off the gold column, but first he had a hole bored into it to ascertain whether it was hollow or not. Juno, however, appeared to Hannibal in a dream and warned that she would blind him in his one good eye if he carried out the theft. On waking, not only did Hannibal heed the warning, but he also had a statuette of a heifer fashioned out of the rock fragments created when the column had been drilled, which was then set upon the top of the column. Once the Carthaginian general was aware of the grave sacrilege that he was about to commit, he not only desisted but also sought to make good the slight that he had afforded the goddess. It was only subsequently that Roman historians turned it into a parable highlighting Hannibal's supposed impiety.

In addition, the Cape Lacinium sanctuary may not have appealed to Hannibal only because of its connections with Juno. One tradition had it that the temple had been built by none other than Hercules. The details of the story also hold other clues as to its Hannibalic provenance. Scholars have long recognized the close parallels between this tale and the claim made by the Greek philosopher Euhemerus, whose ideas had been such a key element of Hannibal's association with Hercules, that on an island in the Indian Ocean he had discovered a golden column on which was carved the most ancient history of the world, and particularly an account of the origins of humankind through the earliest Greek gods. The story of the golden heifer, as a final evocation of the euphemistic creed through which the Carthaginian general had tried to reach out to the Greek world, was as much a testament to the Hannibalic legacy as the inscription that detailed his troop numbers and military campaigns. However, one must imagine that later, under Silenus' skillful pen as he wrote up his account of Hannibal's expedition after its final failure, it became a mournful eulogy to the last great champion of the syncretistic realm of Hercules–Melqart. Long after Hannibal's departure, the Romans remained wary of the sanctuary and the goddess. When the censor Quintus Fulvius Flaccus removed the tiles from the roof of the temple in 174/173 for use on a temple to Fortune that he was building in Rome, the Senate quickly moved to counter this perceived impiety. During a severe carpeting by his senatorial peers, Flaccus was asked, 'Had he considered that he had insufficiently violated the temple, the most revered in that region, one which neither Pyrrhus nor Hannibal had violated, unless he had foully removed its roof and almost torn it down?' After a careful expiation had been carried out, the tiles were returned to the temple–where they were placed in the building, because none of the masons could master how to secure them back on the roof. Roman accounts of a massacre of Italian troops at the sanctuary may well have been aimed at countering Hannibalic claims that the temple of Juno at Cape Lacinium represented the final coordinate of the heroic journey that the Carthaginian general had made over the previous fifteen years. Yet even if the accusation was false, what could not be denied was that, in departing from Italy, Hannibal had left his Italian allies to an uncertain future. Indeed, the extraordinary number of coin hoards found in Bruttium, clearly buried by their owners until better times returned, bear mute but tragic testament to the ominous position of those left behind. In an indication of his lack of trust in the Council of Elders, Hannibal did not proceed directly to Carthage, but camped at the port of Hadrumetum, some 120 kilometers south of the metropolis. He had arrived just in time, because by the spring of 202 the fragile truce with Rome had been broken. When the Carthaginians looted and requisitioned some Roman supply vessels driven ashore by a storm, the Roman envoys sent to demand reparations had been given short shrift, for the Council of Elders had clearly been buoyed by the nearby presence of Hannibal and his troops. The envoys, furthermore, were nearly lynched by a mob and saved only by the timely intervention of the leaders of the anti-Barcid faction, Hasdrubal Haedus and Hanno.

The more extreme elements within the Council of Elders nevertheless then attempted an ambush, and while the envoys' ship managed to escape, several fatalities were inflicted. This deliberate provocation now led Scipio to act decisively. First he summoned his ally the

Numidian king Masinissa to join him with his forces, and then, in a clear attempt to force Hannibal into open battle, he started a brutal campaign of attacking and razing to the ground a number of towns situated in the populous and fertile Medjerda valley, selling their populations into slavery. This ruthless tactic soon bore fruit, and representatives from the Carthaginian Council of Elders implored Hannibal to attack Scipio as soon as possible. Hannibal thus marched north-westward, perhaps with the intention of cutting off Masinissa and his troops before they could join up with Scipio's army. In October 202 he eventually caught up with the Romans at Zama, about five days' march to the south-west of Carthage. Scipio, in a marvelous display of morale-boosting bravado, invited captured Carthaginian scouts sent to reconnoiter the Roman positions to walk freely around his camp and take back their discoveries to their general. This gesture may have been less carefree than it first appears, however, for Scipio relocated his camp to a new position soon after.

With the two armies now making the necessary preparations for combat, Hannibal requested a meeting with Scipio. The Carthaginian, whose enormous experience perhaps already told him that military victory against Scipio's forces was unlikely, tried to negotiate new, milder, terms for a treaty. Scipio, however, confident of a victory on the battlefield, refused. The next morning battle was joined. Although Hannibal's army was more numerous, with now around 50,000 men to Scipio's 29,000, the 6,000 well-trained Numidian cavalry provided by Masinissa gave the Romans a significant advantage. With little cavalry of his own and an untested infantry, Hannibal's battle strategy reflected his rather limited options. Unlike in Italy, where he had often been able to use his advantage in cavalry to encircle the enemy at the wings, at Zama he lined his men up in three lines, with the remnants of his brother Mago's mercenary army in the front rank, a force of Libyan levies and Carthaginian citizens in the second, and his own force of heavily armored veterans in reserve. His tactics would be simple: he would use brute force to drive a way through the center of the Roman army, drawn up in a similar formation of three lines (with the most experienced troops at the rear).

This was certainly not the most sophisticated battle plan, but considering the resources at Hannibal's disposal it probably represented the most realistic option. The lack of coherence within the Carthaginian army was highlighted from the beginning of the battle, for Hannibal merely exhorted and encouraged his own veterans in the third row, and the responsibility for rousing the other groups fell to the captains. In order to make the initial break through the Roman front line, Hannibal relied on a troop of eighty elephants. However, Scipio had already prepared his force for that particular challenge by creating broad corridors through the three massed ranks of his troops. When at last the battle began and the elephants charged, most of those beasts that did not panic and rampage back into their own lines were easily channeled down the lanes that cut through the Roman ranks. Taking advantage of the turmoil, Masinissa's horsemen and the Roman cavalry charged their opposite numbers and drove them from the battlefield. Among the infantry, the fight was far more even-handed, with both sides standing their ground and inflicting heavy losses on the other before eventually the Carthaginian first and second lines were forced back. After Scipio had reordered his troops into one single massed line, the struggle began against Hannibal's 20,000 battle-hardened veterans, who had been kept in reserve by their commander. The two forces proved evenly matched until the returning Roman cavalry attacked the rear of the Carthaginian lines. Many of Hannibal's famed soldiers were killed, with around the same number captured. It was a crippling blow, both for Hannibal himself, who had managed to escape the battleground, and for Carthage. Zama effectively brought the second great war between Rome and Carthage to an end.

Chapter 15: Nothing Lasts Forever

After first fleeing to his base at Hadrumetum, Hannibal then traveled to Carthage for a crisis summit with the Council of Elders. His advice to the assembled grandees was typically blunt: the war was lost, and Carthage's only hope of salvation was now to sue for peace. The Council acted quickly. Ten envoys, including the leaders of the pro-peace party, Hanno and Hasdrubal Haedus, were at once sent to the Romans in a ship decorated with olive branches (the traditional symbols of supplication) and with a herald's caduceus fixed to its prow. Scipio, meeting the ship as his own fleet sailed towards Carthage, ordered the envoys to travel on to Tunes, where he was camped. The peace terms that he proposed there were understandably harsher than those that he had previously offered.

In addition to the previous provisions, Carthage was now forbidden from fighting any wars outside Africa, and even on that continent it had first to seek permission from Rome. The indemnity was now set at 10,000 talents (26,000 kilograms) of silver, to be paid over fifty years—nearly ten times the amount demanded in the terms of the 241 treaty. Moreover, Carthage was to hand over all its war elephants, and its fleet was to be reduced to just ten warships. At Carthage the terms were accepted by the Council of Elders with only one exception. A certain Gisco had stood up to speak against the treaty, but Hannibal, clearly exasperated by this refusal to acknowledge the harsh reality of the situation, manhandled him off the stage. As an indication of the tensions that already existed between Hannibal and many of the elders, the general was forced to apologize for his behavior. The Council nevertheless accepted Hannibal's advice to accept these terms as relatively lenient. And so, towards the end of 202, Carthaginian envoys led by Hasdrubal Haedus traveled to Rome and declared to the Senate their agreement to the peace conditions, before returning to North

Africa, where the treaty was ratified. Carthage's fleet was then dramatically burnt in full view of its citizens, and Latin and Roman deserters were executed. Scipio then embarked his army, as well as 4,000 prisoners of war released by the Carthaginians, and set off for Rome, where he held a magnificent triumph.

As a tribute to his extraordinary achievements, he would forever after be known as 'Africanus'. According to several Roman sources, Hannibal remained in charge of the remnants of his army and kept them occupied by organizing the planting of a huge number of olive groves. By 196 BC, however, he had apparently tired of semi-private life, and had decided to enter the political arena as a Carthaginian magistrate. He would quickly prove himself to be as dynamic a statesman as he was a general. By exposing and attacking the abuses and corruption that had for so long been a hallmark of Carthaginian political life, Hannibal quickly built himself a reputation as a champion of the common citizenry. He successfully proposed a new law which stated that the Tribunal of One Hundred and Four's membership should henceforth be decided by annual election, and that no one should serve consecutive terms. Such a populist move was never likely to have endeared him to the Council of Elders, which he appears to have circumvented entirely. Animosities were further heightened when Hannibal then announced an audit of public revenues, which he would personally oversee.

After conducting a thorough investigation, he supposedly discovered that large amounts of state funds were being lost due to embezzlement by officials. He then declared in the Popular Assembly that if the duties collected on property and port duties were correctly collected there would be enough to pay the indemnity owed to Rome without recourse to extra taxation. Although this must have further boosted Hannibal's popularity among the people of Carthage, the animosity directed at him by the corrupt officials commensurately increased. In adopting such a populist agenda, Hannibal appeared to be following the same political strategy that had so benefited Hamilcar and Hasdrubal Barca nearly forty years previously. Indeed, Hannibal's deliberate use of the Popular Assembly to push his measures through and limit the powers of the broader elite placed him on the well-worn path of Barcid demagogy.

It has been argued that Hannibal was also the driving force behind an ambitious new construction program which witnessed the building of new residential quarters and the great improvement of the city in general. Were some on the Council of Elders worried that these populist reforms were building to a bid for autocratic power? Such concerns would certainly explain the Council's subsequent move, which was to send reports to Rome that Hannibal was secretly negotiating with Antiochus, king of the Seleucid Empire. Antiochus, whose realm stretched from south-eastern Asia Minor

(Turkey) in the west to the kingdom of Bactria (modern Afghanistan) in the east, was now involved in a tense diplomatic confrontation with the Romans over Greece and the Greek cities of western Asia Minor. When Roman envoys subsequently arrived in Carthage to investigate the claims, in 195, Hannibal was forced to flee east, traveling via Tyre and Antioch and thence on to Ephesus, where Antiochus had his court. Paradoxically, accusations that Hannibal was in collusion with Antiochus left the Carthaginian with little option but to seek the king's protection. At the court of Antiochus, Hannibal proposed a daring return to Carthage and a subsequent attack on the Italian peninsula. The dispatch of an agent to arrange a prior Carthaginian rebellion with the Barcids in North Africa spectacularly failed, however, and the Carthaginians, nervous of their new overlords' potential reaction, quickly informed the Roman Senate of Hannibal's machinations. Hannibal had grossly underestimated the degree of support which the once lone voice of Hanno now enjoyed at Carthage, and his attempts to secure an opportunity to make good the failures of the past looked increasingly desperate. Snubbed by his own people, the victor of Cannae now found himself on the fringes of Antiochus' court. Indeed, Antiochus and his advisers must have had serious concerns about the strategy that Hannibal reportedly advocated. According to Livy, his plan was 'always one and the same, that the war should be waged in Italy; Italy would supply both food and soldiers to a foreign enemy; if no disturbance was created there and the Roman people was permitted to use the manpower and resources of Italy for a war outside Italy, neither the king nor any people could be a match for the Romans.' When war between Rome and Antiochus did eventually break out, Hannibal's strategic advice remained equally quixotic and was, unsurprisingly, politely ignored. Hannibal would, however, have one final fleeting taste of military glory. Recognizing that the general's Punic roots would play well with the Phoenician cities of the Levant, he was dispatched by Antiochus to muster and prepare a small fleet of warships.

This Seleucid naval force clashed with the Roman fleet off the coast of Pamphylia in Asia Minor, and for some time the left wing, commanded by Hannibal, managed to hold its own against far more experienced and skilful opponents. Eventually, however, the Seleucid ships were driven back and were effectively blockaded in the port of Side. One can only imagine Hannibal's shock and sorrow to see Carthaginian ships among the Roman fleet. With the Seleucids eventually defeated at Magnesia in Asia Minor in 189, Hannibal spent the rest of his life wandering the courts of the Hellenistic East. Although his exact itinerary remains a matter of conjecture, anecdotal evidence places him variously on Crete and in Armenia (where he supposedly helped to build a new city). His final refuge, however, was Bithynia, a kingdom in north-western Asia Minor. Here he is said to have continued his career as an urban planner, by creating a new capital, as well as developing the tactic of hurling snake-filled pots on to the decks of enemy ships during battles at sea. Despite the services which he provided for the Bithynian king Pruisas, Hannibal was nonetheless a diplomatic liability. When, in 183, the Roman general Titus Quinctius Flaminius visited Bithynia, he upbraided the king when Hannibal's presence was discovered. Pruisas, concerned about the repercussions of shielding so controversial a guest at a time when Roman power was growing in the region, immediately resolved to surrender Hannibal. When Bithynian soldiers blocked off all exits from his hideout on the coast, Hannibal, realizing that escape was impossible, took the poison that he always carried with him, thus avoiding the humiliation of capture.

As he died, according to Livy, he condemned the Romans for their vindictiveness, impiety and lack of faith. Thus the life of Carthage's greatest son reached its dramatic end.

Conclusion

Hannibal and Scipio were two men linked together. Each was the only military commander in their time who was an equal match in open battle. Each was a hero and often times Savior of their people, but ultimately unappreciated. They led their nations through times of war, helped to rebuild, and thrived despite the odds. In the case of Hannibal, the Carthaginians grew weary of his family's influence. After the end of the second Punic war, he rebuilt Carthage and led it to even greater economic prosperity. But he would not find peace or safety within his homelands. He would be forced to flee, as they would not stand with him.

Scipio similarly felt unappreciated. He was accused on more than one occasion of accepting bribes that were against the interests of Rome. Each time he would defend himself showing his service record in declaring his deeds, and finally would outright deny the claims against him. He eventually retired from public life and chose to become a simple farmer in the countryside. All the way until his death he remained bitter of his countrymen's ingratitude.

The final sad years of Hannibal's life might be viewed as a parable of Roman vengefulness, but in fact his fate had been largely decided by his own countrymen. Tired of his egotistical maneuverings to undermine the Carthaginian political system at a time of distinct instability, the majority of the Council of Elders had been desperate to be rid of him. Hannibal's political failures and misjudgments become more understandable, however, when one considers that, beyond the network of loyalties and relationships that were part of his Barcid inheritance, he was a stranger to the Carthaginian elite, in a way that Hamilcar and Hasdrubal Barca, who had spent their formative years in the city, had not been. With his restless energy and inability to tolerate dissent, Hannibal therefore took his place among that long line of military heroes who would prove themselves singularly ill-suited for political office. In Rome, the news of Hannibal's death received a mixed reaction.

According to Plutarch, some approved of Flaminius' action, because they 'thought that Hannibal, as long as he lived, was a consuming fire which needed only to be fanned; for when he was not in his prime, they said, it was not his body nor his arm that had been formidable against the Romans, but his ability and experience coupled with his deep bitterness and hostility'. Others, however, 'thought that the conduct of Titus [Flaminius] was cruel: for it had killed Hannibal when he was like a bird allowed to live a tame and harmless life because he was too old to fly and without tail feathers'. Leading the latter party was Scipio Africanus—a fact which some have seen as a reflection of the Roman's high regard for his erstwhile opponent. Scipio was, however, far too much of a pragmatist to allow such sentimentality to cloud his judgment The Roman hero, who knew the political situation in Carthage better than most, knew that Hannibal now had no chance of rousing a rebellion against the might of Rome. It could nevertheless be argued that both sides were right. Although Hannibal was certainly no longer a threat in Carthaginian terms, at the royal courts of the Hellenistic kings his name must surely have still conjured up the seductive image of resistance to Rome. Hannibal himself had been quick to realize this, and had soon produced at least one anti-Roman tract—written in the early 180s, and in the form of a speech addressed to the people of Rhodes—in which he outlined the barbarous outrages committed in Asia Minor by the Roman general Gnaeus Manlius Vulso, with the clear intention of turning his audience against Roman power.

Others too were anxious to appropriate the influence still attached to Hannibal's name. In the same period a fake letter, supposedly written by the Carthaginian general after Cannae, was in circulation. In it 'Hannibal' announced his famous victory and foretold that a rebellion among the Greeks would bring an end to Roman domination of the eastern Mediterranean. For many at Rome, therefore, the mere existence of Hannibal, not just at the court of the enemy, but simply as a symbol of resistance, may well have demanded his death. The reasons for Rome's pursuit of Hannibal, however, extended well beyond any threat that he himself might still represent, for the divisive feelings which he inspired within the Roman Senate made his pursuit a matter of internal politics also. The persecution of Hannibal was therefore also the persecution of his nemesis turned protector Scipio Africanus. The fate of the two men had always been intimately intertwined, and in the wake of his victories in North Africa the Roman hero had found himself similarly isolated by the political establishment at home. In Rome itself, although a number of his supporters had won elections to high political office, Scipio had achieved very little of worth during his own second consulship, of 194, and he found his ambitions increasingly frustrated by a growing band of opponents in the Senate. Indeed, Scipio's inability to transfer the success that he had enjoyed on the battlefield to the political sphere appeared closely to mirror the disappointments that Hannibal had suffered in Carthage.

For Scipio, decline had begun when he and his brother Lucius were recalled to Rome from their victorious military campaign against Antiochus. Their political enemies, led by Marcus Porcius Cato, had persuaded the Senate to pass a bill whereby consuls should hold commands for only a single year, and had then attempted to prosecute several of their friends and supporters. The Scipios then found themselves under attack when they were called to account for 500 talents of silver given to them by Antiochus as a term of the armistice. Scipio Africanus did not help himself by haughtily tearing up the campaign account books in full view of the Senate. Sensing weakness, Cato and his supporters continued to press the Scipios, and the more the latter refused to account for the money, the more suspicions grew. Finally, in 184, Scipio Africanus suffered the indignity of being prosecuted in the courts on the charge of taking bribes from Antiochus. Realizing that his enemies were in the ascendant, Scipio now opted to leave Rome for his estates at Liternum in Campania, and Cato, his political aims achieved, let the prosecution drop. Within a year, however, the great hero of Zama died a broken man. That the downfalls of these two great men should follow such similar trajectories is perhaps unsurprising when one considers not only the congruities in their respective political strategies, but also the political systems within which they operated. Scipio, the great hero and a powerful symbol of Roman triumph over Carthage, soon became a dangerous, destabilizing force within a system that centered on the elaborate fiction that all members of its Senate were equal.

Hannibal's presence within the political scene at Carthage had proved similarly problematic. His populist reforms, and the concomitant contempt which he showed for fellow members of the Council, presented him to others as a potential autocrat. Confronted with a living hero in their very midst—a hero whose very stature threatened to dwarf those institutions he had been charged to protect—both the Carthaginian Council and the Roman Senate had acted decisively to isolate their former champions. The last age of heroes had come to an emphatic close.

These two men fight for their homelands and their beliefs. They gave all they had to their people, and ultimately received nothing in return when it truly mattered. The legacy of the Barca family came to an end. Rome's vengeance against him and against Carthage was so complete that few records have survived. They destroyed statues, burned buildings, and razed temples to the ground. All comprehensive records that remain are from Roman sources, the majority of biased. It is enough to make one wonder what things could be learned about this great man in the Homeland he defended if the record still existed.

Other books available by author on Kindle, paperback and audio

History's Greatest Military Commanders: The Brilliant Military Strategies of Hannibal, Alexander The Great, Sun Tzu, Julius Caesar, Napoleon Bonaparte, And 30 Other Historical Commanders

The Rise And Fall Of The Roman Empire: Life, Liberty, And The Death Of The Republic